*"Guide me in your truth and teach me,
for you are God my Savior,
and my hope is in you all day long."*

~Psalm 25:5

A JOURNEY TO
HOPE

Stories That Inspire

2018

Copyright © 2018
Tribute Publishing, LLC
Frisco, Texas

Tribute Publishing, LLC

A Journey to Hope
First Edition August 2018

All Worldwide Rights Reserved
ISBN: 978-0-9998358-3-8

All Rights Reserved. No part of this book may be reproduced, stored in a retrieval system, or transmitted, in any form, or by any means, electronic, mechanical, recorded, photocopied, or otherwise, without the prior written permission of the copyright owner, except by a reviewer who may quote brief passages in a review.

In God We Trust

*"Trust in the LORD with all your heart;
do not depend on your own understanding.
Seek his will in all you do,
and he will show you which path to take."*

~Proverbs 3:5-6

Contents

Introduction xi

Chapter 1 – Your Life Is a Gift to You 1

Chapter 2 – Experiencing God in My Ignorance 17

Chapter 3 – God Was There 33

Chapter 4 – On the Other End 53

**Chapter 5 – The Path to Impact,
                 Significance, and Success** 77

Chapter 6 – Love Is the Answer 95

Chapter 7 – Strategic Storm 113

Chapter 8 – Reconnecting with Your Why 137

Final Thoughts 161

About Mike Rodriguez 165

Introduction

*M*any times in my life I have been humbled by opportunities to witness God's blessing and miracles; whether in my own life or through the life of a family member, friend or someone else. I cannot and will not profess to know how or why God does what He does, He is after all, God. However, I do know that He is present, and we can experience a glimpse of His love and compassion if we only get to know Him through His son Jesus.

I decided to publish this book because I knew there were others like me who had a story to tell about God's amazing work. Others who had witnessed first-hand his blessings. Normal people like me and like you that had a story of faith to share.

The contributing authors in this book were brave enough to share their own stories and insights. They did this with the hope that other people, like you, would find something to take away. Something that would inspire you to make the important changes in your life. To understand that what you are going through does not define you but can certainly refine you to start living with hope. You can do it; however, you must be willing to believe, take action, and start pursuing your greatest purpose. I would like to tell you that it is going to be easy, but it is not. I would like to say that there is nothing special about the contributors to this book, but that would also not be true. Yet, it would also be false for you to believe that there is nothing special about you, too.

You were created with precision, purpose, and your own unique talents. You were also given the ability to know, act on, and use those talents to become greater and stronger in your own way for God's purposes.

Just accept, remember, and most importantly believe this, "I can do all things through Christ, who strengthens me." Philippians 4:13 (*NKJV*). As I always say, "Through faith and action, ALL things are possible."

Now, let's get YOU started on your journey to hope.

Mike Rodriguez

*"It's not that you have lost hope,
you are simply looking in the wrong direction."*
- Mike Rodriguez

Chapter 1

Your Life Is a Gift to You
By Mike Rodriguez

Where you are in your life right now is only temporary.
It's up to you to let it become permanent.

This applies to all situations and to all people. Whether you are on top of the world right now, facing a tragic loss or even if you feel that you are just existing, it is only temporary. If you are at a point in your life that is not "where" you expected or "what" you expected, that is certainly understandable. It is, however, up to you to let where you are, become permanent. Life doesn't always present good situations, nor are they easy. Regardless of how you view where you are, you must believe that what is happening, is happening for a reason. When facing a tough time or going through a bad situation, let yourself feel whatever emotions you are going through, but don't let them overtake you. Tough times will not last when God is in control.

Most of the challenges that I have lived through, when I trace them back, were usually a result of the

Chapter 1 – Your Life Is a Gift to You

consequences of my decisions (or indecisions) which preceded my actions. Yet, I have also learned that God places us in situations or allows situations to happen, for us to get through, so He can get through to us. Situations that you are in may not make sense to you today, but they will later.

All of life's experiences serve a higher purpose - to bring us closer to God. He is indeed mysterious and when we seek to understand Him from a human perspective, nothing that has happened or that will happen in our lives could ever make sense, because God is not human. He is the almighty creator of the universe!

In fact, He tells us:

> "For My thoughts are not your thoughts,
> Nor are your ways My ways," declares the LORD.
> "For as the heavens are higher than the earth,
> So are My ways higher than your ways
> And My thoughts than your thoughts.
> – Isaiah 55:8-9

I find that most of us rationalize with and analyze our creator, based on what we feel, want, need or hope to happen. This is where we get side-tracked on our journey through life, especially when we are going through tough times. We must learn to understand that in life, we are either moving closer towards God or we are moving further from Him. Let me clarify that He is always with us and never leaves us. Regardless of where we are in life, what we are doing or what we are going through, he is always there.

Chapter 1 – Your Life Is a Gift to You

When we do things to move further away from God, this means that we are choosing to think, speak or act in a way that is not compatible with allowing Him to go to work in our lives. This usually involves us doing something that we shouldn't be doing, having a lack of faith in general or just living our lives in our own way, according to the world and our will. Awareness of our selfishness, creates an awareness of change.

I will be the first one to agree that initially, it will seem very difficult to start making changes in your life that put God first in everything. However, once you make the decision, you will find that living with faith and a positive attitude to change, requires as much energy and effort as living with doubt, worry, fear and uncertainty. Then, once you start trusting Him more, you realize that you can change.

For a large part of my life, although I was a Christian, I had let the ways of the world influence my thoughts, actions and words, which impacted my life plans, which made me look like everyone in this world. We do live in this world, but we should not become like this world. We need to work every day to include Him, not as an add-on, but as "The One." This doesn't mean that you won't have doubts, worries and fears, but it does mean that you can have peace and faith through your tough times. Your life does have a plan, a better plan, and there is a light at the end of the tunnel.

I know that God has always been with me, all the time. There has never been a doubt in my mind. However, I kept Him at a distance to make sure that I didn't feel too

Chapter 1 – Your Life Is a Gift to You

bad about my behavior. At times, when I was strong in my faith, I would let my light shine and I felt wonderful. However, when I wasn't strong, when I wasn't living right or when I was just not being happy, I would make sure that I was keeping Him at a reasonable distance. I did this, so I could still feel good about myself. As if He didn't know.

The explanation that I can give is that it was like I was walking through a very long tunnel made of glass, like at an aquarium. The tunnel represented my life's journey. I would walk down the middle of the tunnel and God was ALWAYS walking at the same pace as me, right next to me, but always on the outside of the glass. Not because He wanted to be there, but because I wouldn't let Him in. The glass allowed me to see Him and be assured of His presence, but it also served the purpose of keeping Him from being too close in my life. I wanted His presence, but not His conviction over me, primarily because I was ashamed of my actions. To others, I am also ashamed to say, that I didn't want to come across as "religious." Ironically, when I had low points in my life, I would become angry with God for not being with me. How silly was that thinking, because He was always there. It was only when I learned to become obedient and change my life, that I finally learned and made the decision to break down that glass wall. We would no longer be separated. I would welcome Him because I was no longer ashamed, and I was empowered by this new amazing and peaceful presence.

His love is unconditional. There is nothing that you have done or that you can do to mess it up. Accept this as a

Chapter 1 – Your Life Is a Gift to You

truth and remind yourself of this when you are feeling low. When you are down, it's easy to feel hopeless and abandoned. Just know that you are never alone and hope is always present. You only have to believe and seek.

In my new walk, following His plan, He is still with me and I can still see Him; but now I can feel, know and have a completely different kind of love with Him. There are no barriers between us. The reality is that His love has never changed. Mine has.

Most of us live our lives this same way, by using God as a convenience. Sometimes we only call on Him when we are at our darkest moments. It is a truth that no one wants to admit. This is usually apparent when we face some kind of bad or life-changing event, usually with undesirable consequences. He is always there for us, but sometimes we are only there, obediently, when we feel the need or when it is convenient for us. This mindset is counter-productive to building the kind of relationship that we need. Turning away from the ways of the world is very hard indeed.

God made you and me and He knows everything about us and everything that will happen in our lives. We have been prepared for every situation that we will encounter, even when we feel like we can't make it. He loves us unconditionally and wants us all of us, all of the time, good and bad. He wants you to call on Him when you are at your lowest, but He also asks that you praise Him at your highest and all times in between! Give thanks and praise during your good times, but also find the strength to give praise and

Chapter 1 – Your Life Is a Gift to You

thanks during difficulties, even when you don't understand what is happening or why it is happening. Of course, this is easier said than done, but it is, in fact, your choice. During good times it's easy to give thanks, yet during difficult times it is equally important to give thanks to God. You are going through whatever it is that you are going through for a reason. He is with you and you must believe that the situation ultimately serves a purpose for His plans for your life.

Life's Standards

There is one constant in life: change will happen. Your life involves people, routines, circumstances, events and God's will. With almost all of these, you have limited power in controlling what happens. What you can control is your faith and your attitude about how you respond to what happens to you. You can also control your decision to act.

Circumstances will happen, and things will not always be in your favor; no one plans on leaving the house and getting in a wreck, but it happens. You might go into work and find out that you have suddenly been laid off, or you might get the surprise gift of a promotion. Things will happen to you, but they are not the standards in your life. They are merely events happening according to events, people, circumstances and of course, God's will.

To better explain how you should view this as you progress in life, I have created a graph. As you look at the graph, you will notice that there are three lines. These lines

Chapter 1 – Your Life Is a Gift to You

represent measurements, highs and lows, of where you are when events happen in your life, with examples.

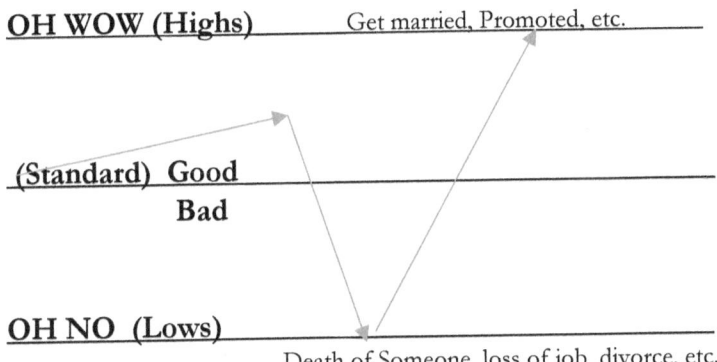

The Bottom Line, the "OH NO" line, represents the challenges that you face in your life. Anything from the "Bad" line down to this line measures everything negative that happens in your life.

The Top Line is the "OH WOW" line. Anything from the "Good" line which is above "The Standard" line, up to this line, would measure positive events that happen in your life.

The Middle Line is the "Standard" line. This represents life as a regular day without any major events.

The Bottom Line, the "OH NO" line, represents the challenges that you face in your life. Anything from the "Bad" line down to this line measures everything negative that happens in your life.

If you have a tragic event, say a death in your family, you can see that this can drop you well below your life standard to the "OH NO" line. Likewise, if you have a major victory,

Chapter 1 – Your Life Is a Gift to You

like getting promoted, or getting engaged, you can be propelled up to the "OH WOW" line.

In life, you are either moving forward and up or forward and down. We don't move backwards. We simply choose to stay at certain levels depending on the circumstances that we encounter. Right now, you are probably saying, I'm not choosing to stay unhappy or mad, things have happened to me!

Yes, things may have happened, but you must learn to adjust and choose to move on. This mindset becomes more relevant when facing a difficult challenge. We might become depressed, create a negative attitude, and feel that our life is meaningless. We might even feel that we are not even capable of moving forward. This is the point where we stop living and stay low on the chart. The thought of your life being worthless is simply not true, but this is how we get into trouble; we stop living for and trusting in God's plans.

You must remember that God is always with you and He wants you to focus on serving Him! You must also believe this and say this to yourself: All things are temporary; God is in control.

During good times, we tend to recognize, rejoice and praise God when we are above the "standard" line. The challenge with this mindset is that you might get an unrealistic expectation of life and things might appear tougher when you fall again. Enjoy where you are, but understand the nature of the event that you are rejoicing in.

Chapter 1 – Your Life Is a Gift to You

Remember, ALL things in life are temporary, except for God.

When we fall below the standard line, this is when we start to doubt and question God. We might even become angry. When we get to this point, sometimes we tend to stay there and hold ourselves below life's standards. We might even feel like we have the right to stay down there. We don't.

We must learn to think and believe that everything happens for a reason. A great event is simply that; a great event. It isn't permanent or the new standard in your life. Likewise, a bad event is simply that; a bad event. Neither of them becomes the new standard in your life. You will only stay at a place that you choose to stay at, and you will only stay there if you choose to stay there.

Life's events do not happen to define us, they happen to "refine" us. We must keep moving forward and we must keep moving upwards.

"God allows us to go through challenges,
Not to DEFINE us, but to REFINE us."

Success

We often equate success with being happy. Please know that this isn't necessarily true. Your happiness is 100%

Chapter 1 – Your Life Is a Gift to You

dependent on you, not your circumstances or things. When you consider that "things" do not carry emotion; you can determine that your emotions about "things" are really a direct result of your own conscious or subconscious decisions. If you are an unhappy person, regardless of how successful you become, or how many things you buy, you are still you, so you will probably remain unhappy.

The questions to ask yourself are:

1. How do I define success?
2. How do I define happiness?
3. How will I attain either one?

Success can and usually has different meanings to different people. It is important to find out what motivates you, what your goals are and what you were called to accomplish. You are your own unique person. God made you for and with a purpose. Sometimes situations that you are in can motivate you and can prompt you to become better. Success can and will have different meanings to different people. Some people measure success by money, others by fame and some by material possessions. However, those may not be the true measurements of success for you. If your goal is to be a better husband or wife and you have taken steps to make this happen and your family recognizes it, then you are indeed a success. If you choose to improve your life and your career, and you do, then you are successful.

Chapter 1 – Your Life Is a Gift to You

Happiness

Happiness, on the other hand, is a state of mind, based on your reaction or response to something. Sometimes it might be a very difficult choice for you to be happy, especially if you are going through a hardship. Being sad and staying sad is a difficult mindset to come out of, so you must look inside of yourself, (not outside to things) to find and remember your own happiness. You can have many material things and personal relationships, but if you are not content with your own life, you will still not be happy.

Happiness is not offered by others, nor is it found in things. Buying a material possession or celebrating an event can certainly create joy, but true internal happiness is based on your decision to follow Christ.

Appreciating where you are in life and what you have materialistically, is a big start. Understand that purchasing more items does not bring true happiness. You may not live or work where you want to and that's fine, but to move to the next level, you must learn to appreciate what you have today. God will provide blessings in your life in many ways, but how can He continue to bless you with more opportunity if you cannot appreciate where you already are and what you already have?

When you understand that every situation in your life is merely a stepping stone and part of God's plan, then you start to understand the value and importance of everything in your life. Everything that you do and every situation that

Chapter 1 – Your Life Is a Gift to You

you encounter, is a step that must be taken in order to get to the top of the next step. When you lose the importance of a life's step due to a setback, it will keep you from moving forward and moving closer towards God's plan for your life.

There is a plan for your life, a better plan.

We are born perfect in God's eyes, fully prepared to succeed, but along the way, we lose sight of whose we are and what we're capable of achieving through trusting in Him. Life happens to us and we start engaging in bad or unhealthy things. We might begin to abuse alcohol, drugs, food or something else. We might start getting angry, depressed, or create unhealthy addictions, thoughts or actions. Sometimes we completely redefine who we think we are, due to the confusion and deception in this world. However, God's message is very clear: He has already equipped you for His plan. You just need to trust in Him, accept Him and accept who He created you to be.

When you were born, do you remember that tag made of flesh attached to your side? You know, the one that said, "addict," "depressed," "anger issues," "fearful," "worried," "confused" or something else that was negative?

No, you say? You don't remember having that or even being born with an extra flesh tag with a negative description of yourself? Of course not, because it wasn't there.

The reason it wasn't there, is because God never put it there! This is the part where you might say, but Mike, I do

Chapter 1 – Your Life Is a Gift to You

have a defining negative characteristic and it is a part of me, but I've always been that way! This is where I tell you that you are wrong. God never gave you any negative defining characteristics. That was all your doing.

Living in a world dominated by sin, causes us to sin. Sometimes, we can sin so much and for so long that we can get confused and accept the sin as our own identity. We can confuse what we DO, as who we are. I challenge you to accept and believe that the things you DO, really aren't who you are. I'm not talking about shirking responsibility for your actions, I am talking about separating what God made you to be, versus what you have added to your life through what you DO. If you are doing things you shouldn't be doing, stop doing them! Once you stop doing those things, you will remove from your life what you brought in or introduced. God never intended those things to be there in the first place.

Sometimes, we do negative and sinful things for so long that we can cover ourselves in those things, hiding who we truly are. When diamonds are mined from the earth, the seekers can be deceived as they sort through thick chunks of carbon. However, if they can keep their eyes on the prize, not on the nasty carbon, the seekers can and usually will find the brilliant gems inside, covered by the years of darkness. It can be difficult to sort through thick layers of dark decay.

It requires great work to remove the layers of carbon to reveal the brilliance of the beautiful diamond inside.

Chapter 1 – Your Life Is a Gift to You

Our lives with Christ are similar to mining diamonds.

God has given us His brilliant, shining light to be found inside, just like a brilliant and precious diamond is found embedded with layers of black, hardened carbon. The challenge is that some of us have hidden the brilliant light within, by covering ourselves with layers of dark carbon, represented by years of sinful nature, negative actions, and habits. Some of us have been sinning for so long that we have falsely accepted the layers of carbon as a part of who we are. When we do this, we allow the layers of darkness to prevent God's brilliant light within us from shining to the rest of the world, assuming we have accepted His light: Jesus.

The great news is that although you may not feel like you can remove the years of negativity or darkness that you may be trapped in, God loves you and He can! He makes all things new! He can help you remove the years of negative and sinful things that have been hiding His light inside of you if you only trust in Him!

Yes, you and God started your life journey and it will be just you and God who will end your life journey together, if you know Him. Will you be prepared to give an account of what you did according to His plans for your life?

You can be prepared…. right now.

Here is how:

The Bible says that the only way to know God is through Jesus. In fact, Jesus said, "I am the way, the truth, and the life. No one can come to the Father except through me." John 14: 6.

Chapter 1 – Your Life Is a Gift to You

This means that by asking Jesus into your life, you can know God, be forgiven of your sins and have eternal life in Heaven. In your own words, pray and repent of your sins and confess that you believe Jesus died for your sins on the cross. Acknowledge Jesus Christ as your Lord and Savior and ask Him into your heart. Tell Him you want to start new.

If you said this prayer on your own free will right now, then congratulations, you have been saved and you are fully equipped to start a better plan, God's plan! Praise God.

However, you need to continue to do your part and live your life in a way that honors God, by getting into a Christian Church that teaches about Jesus and the Bible

Now go forth and make your life exceptional!

- Mike Rodriguez

www.MikeRodriguezInternational.com

Chapter 1 – Your Life Is a Gift to You

Chapter 2

Experiencing God in My Ignorance
By Nathaniel Thomas Varghese

"If the God of the Bible causes his followers to suffer and be mistreated, I do not want to serve him."

As I grew up, I watched my family being persecuted for Christ. The anti-Christian religious leaders in India threatened to harm or kill them if they would not stop sharing the gospel. When I was a junior in high school, the local newspaper published the names of my family members who were demanded to be beheaded. This threat shook up my family. Later that year, I saw thousands of people break through the gate of the Christian school that my family directed. They could not stand that we were sharing the gospel. When I heard the commotion, I came out of our house behind the school and watched the scene, hiding in the corner. They burned the buses down and started throwing stones at the windows. I could hear glass shattering all over the place. The mob was running through the school and destroying it.

At that moment, when I thought that this would be the end of our lives, I decided that I cannot serve the God that my parents served. How can this God, who makes his disciples go through pain and persecution, be loving?

Chapter 2 – Experiencing God in My Ignorance

Though my family clung to their faith, the questions in my mind never stopped. My parents taught me that God was loving, caring, and compassionate. This God was not loving and caring for my family. How could I serve a God like this?

When I finished high school, I decided to go to college to get a degree in business management. My dad was a pastor and most of my relatives were involved in ministry, but I wanted to choose a career that involved God as little as possible. I graduated in three years, ready to work towards becoming a successful businessman.

After I graduated, I applied for jobs in the business world. I received many job offers and I accepted a position in the Finance/Banking sector in South India. It was an incredible opportunity that would line me up for a great career. I loved my work, and as I began to work up the corporate ladder, I loved it even more. I enjoyed going to work every day, and I was in line for even more promotions.

Growing up, when my Mom talked about her faith, she was often emotional, and I never understood it. She would start crying as she would pray, "God, how could you save a sinner like me?" Although I had more interest in God when I had been baptized during my sophomore year in high school, seeing the persecution my family went through hardened my heart against Him. When I was twenty-six, three years into my career at the Bank, I was attending a worship service at church and was convicted of my sin. I had thought that I could just give minimal recognition to God and be a decently good person to be saved. The pastor was preaching that God does not save us on our own qualifications. Christ says, "Believe in me for salvation." (Romans 10:9-10) He does not say, "If you are a good

Chapter 2 – Experiencing God in My Ignorance

person, I will save you." I was starting to get emotional and I did not like that, so as I sat in my pew I prayed, "God, I'm a tough guy. If you can make me cry, you just try it." That day I cried like a baby. I had tried to ignore the fact that I was rebelling against God, but at that moment, I could not hide anymore. I gave my life to Christ that day and trusted his grace instead of my own works.

Even though my heart towards God had changed, I still was pursuing my career at the Bank. After about a year, God suddenly gave me a restlessness with my current course in life. One day I was happy to go to work, the next day I was reluctant. I was confused; I was enjoying my career and had everything I wanted. But each day I went to work, I started to become more discontent.

I finally contacted my uncle, the president of the orphan ministry my family works with. I confessed in my email to him, "I do not know what I am going through… but I think I want to serve God." My uncle was thrilled to hear this because my whole family knew I had wanted nothing to do with the ministry up to this point. He invited me to come up to North India to visit him at a pastors' conference. As I traveled, I was torn between my success in my job and everything I had worked for and God's call on my heart to serve him. When I met my uncle, he listened to what I had to say. Then he simply responded, "I would like you to set up an orphanage in North India."

Without hesitation I responded, "Alright. Sounds like fun!"

I did not know what I was in for or what God was doing, but I was all in. Caring for orphans sounds like fun, why not? I traveled back to South India and resigned from

Chapter 2 – Experiencing God in My Ignorance

my job. My boss and coworkers were shocked. I did not know how to even begin to explain my reasons to them. As I finished my time there, I became a laughing stock in the office. They thought I was out of my mind to resign from my career. They implored me to stay. They could not understand why I would leave when I had such a great job and future.

When my parents heard about my decision to quit my job, they were concerned if I was making this choice rashly. To be honest, I was worried as well. What if this idea to start an orphanage was just an emotional decision? What if when the heat of ministry came, I would just change my mind? I had no idea what I was getting into, but I knew I had to follow God's call on my heart.

My uncle sent me to a campus that had previously been an orphanage. A militant group that was persecuting Christians had completely shut down the orphanage years before because they did not want the gospel to spread in that part of India. The building and land was a beautiful campus for the establishment, but it was currently abandoned because of the persecution. As my decision to restart this children's home became real, I prayed, "Alright God, I will start this orphanage. I have no clue what I'm doing, but I'll start it."

In the beginning, the work was certainly fun. I interviewed and hired local staff to restore the facility and to keep the home running once we had children. As we worked, we had daily meetings for how to get the orphanage up and running again. The next step was to get the permits from the local government office. On the day that I went, the official who issued the licenses was busy, so I left and returned the

Chapter 2 – Experiencing God in My Ignorance

next day. On the next day, I was told he was out, but I could see through the window that he was in his office! When the staff told me he was unable to take appointments, I would wait outside his office while other people who had come after me were called in. As I kept coming back day after day, the official would either avoid me or send me away to return with yet another document. I tried to reason with the office that this orphan home would only help the community, but to no avail. I had submitted all the required paperwork, but they seemed to have no intention of allowing a Christian organization into their community. I was discouraged and started to despair. If God wanted me to start this orphanage, could he not help me get one simple permit? As I waited long hours, God brought Luke 11:5-13 to my mind, "Ask and it will be given to you; seek and you will find; knock and the door will be opened to you." So I kept knocking.

Finally, one day, the official granted the permit! He was tired of seeing me, so he accepted my paperwork just to get rid of me.

Immediately we started adopting kids into the orphanage. Some of the boys that came had been in the orphanage before it had been shut down. Many of these kids were living on the streets and begging to survive or were taken care of by relatives who could not adequately provide for them. After a month, we had adopted as many boys as we had the resources for: forty boys from two to ten years old.

I directed the home and lived in the orphanage with the boys. It was fun to see them getting up early and lining up for breakfast before they were sent off to school. They had never had this opportunity before in their life, and

Chapter 2 – Experiencing God in My Ignorance

suddenly their lifestyle included food, clothing, and shelter. It meant a lot to them, and I could see it on their faces. Every evening I would go out and play cricket and soccer with the kids. Every morning and evening we would come together to worship God. Each day started and ended with prayer. The boys called me "Dad" and I was filled with joy that I had never experienced before.

The God Who Saves

One day, I hosted about twenty Bible students who had traveled from another part of India. They brought about two thousand Gideon New Testaments, and we were going to pass them out and evangelize on the streets in New Delhi. We went out, and as we handed the New Testaments out to whoever would take them, we told everyone, "This is the good news that God brought you, please read it!" We were excited because everyone we approached was taking the Bibles.

However, it did not go without resistance. I have to admit, I am not very tall, so when a six-foot-six-inch Indian man leading several other men walked directly towards us, I got nervous. The leader demanded, "Who is in charge of this?" When they saw that I was the leader, he grabbed me by my collar and pushed me up against the wall. He started to interrogate me, "Who gave you permission to preach Jesus in this area?"

In this area, the government was fiercely persecuting Christians. It was illegal to even share the gospel. The men started telling the people on the street, "Everyone who has a Bible, throw it at his face." In India, we show respect for God's Word by cherishing it. We would not just throw it

Chapter 2 – Experiencing God in My Ignorance

around as if it was a piece of newspaper, so I begged the people on the street not to throw the Bibles, but to just give them back to me.

The group of men kept pushing me and demanding who it was that gave me permission until I told them I did not have permission. When they saw that I had students with me who also had been converted from other religious backgrounds to Christianity, they became even more violent. The students bravely confirmed that they had once been Hindu, but now believed in Jesus.

The leader started making calls on his cell phone and I heard him say, "Bring swords. We will chop this Christian's head off to show everyone that Christians cannot preach the gospel."

Crowds started to assemble at the scene as the men shouted to everyone that they were going to kill me. My heart was beating faster than it had ever before. I was terrified. I had never feared death before, but that was because I had never seen it so close. At that moment, I realized that this was going to be my last day alive.

As the group waited for reinforcements with swords, they grabbed up the Bibles and demanded of me, "There is something in this book about God commanding the Israelites to kill everyone who does not believe in Him." He flipped through the New Testament trying to find a passage that proved his point, but he instead came to a passage that talked about Jesus having compassion for people. Even though I was terrified, I started smiling. I cannot explain it. At that moment, the Holy Spirit brought Matthew 5:10 into my mind: "Blessed are those who are persecuted for righteousness sake, for theirs is the kingdom of heaven" and

Chapter 2 – Experiencing God in My Ignorance

peace flooded into my soul. Paul wrote, "For me to live is Christ, to die is gain." If this was going to be my last day, that meant that I was going to meet my Savior. I also knew that my death would not be in vain. God uses the blood of His martyrs to build His church (Tertullian).

When the officer that had been called in drove up, he grabbed my collar and struck me against the wall again as he threatened, "This is your last warning! If I see you in this area again, I will personally be the one to chop your head off." Then he let me go. A last warning had never been so sweet to me. To this day I have no idea why he released me. In the political climate in India, he could have performed this execution. I knew it was God's work to keep me alive longer for his purposes.

While I was grateful for that narrow escape, I was at peace with God's plan for my life. As I walked back to the orphanage, I knew that if God called me home in a way like that, I was, and still am, ready to die.

The God Who Answers

One day, one of my staff unexpectedly knocked on my office door. When he came into my office, he told me that we had only two days left of food. I replied, "Don't worry, everything will be fine," as my mind started racing.

I still had some savings from my banking job, so I decided to use it for food for the orphanage. This sustained us for quite some time, but eventually, my savings ran out and there was nothing else I could do.

When the knock came on my office door again, I knew we were in trouble. My staff told me, "Sir, we have just a few days of food left for the kids." I did not know what to

Chapter 2 – Experiencing God in My Ignorance

say to him. In just two or three days, we would have nothing left to feed the kids. I could feel anxiety and tension in my whole body. I had a few local supporters that would provide food and money for the orphanage from time to time. I asked them for extra support, but as I left each office or home empty-handed when they could not help, I grew discouraged.

Sometimes it seems like when one thing falls apart, everything falls apart. My savings were gone. My supporters could not provide any help. I had no other options. I started to pray, "God please help us, please provide for Your children."

In the evening, when we had just enough food for the next day's breakfast, I gathered the children and told them the truth, "Kids, tomorrow will be your last breakfast. I don't know what to do, Dad does not have anything else to give you. Please pray."

The kids stood there and were still smiling. I thought that maybe they were not understanding, but I realized that somehow, they were able to have joy in this circumstance. That night as I walked through the rooms, I saw the kids crying and praying. I listened as one boy prayed, "God, Dad does not have money, so we don't have food to eat. He did not have to take care of us, but he chose to take care of us, and he is in this situation today because of us. Please provide." As I walked back to my room, my eyes filled with tears. When I lay down on my bed, all I had left was a small prayer, "God, maybe you don't want to hear my prayer, but please hear these orphans' prayer. Please, please provide."

Chapter 2 – Experiencing God in My Ignorance

The next day we ate breakfast, which was all the food remaining in the house. Then I sent the kids to school like normal. I had no other ideas as I wandered back to my office.

As I sat there, I heard a big military truck pull onto the campus. Immediately my mind flashed back to years ago when militants had driven their trucks into my school and attacked it. I also knew that the police had come in similar trucks to seize this very orphanage under false accusations years ago. My pulse quickened, and fear came over my whole body. Two military officers got out of the truck, approached me, and asked, "Who is in charge of this orphanage?"

Everything inside me wanted to answer that someone else, anyone else, was in charge. Resignedly, I answered the officer, "I am the one in charge." My mind wondered, what was I doing here. I had failed.

When the officer heard that I was in charge, he politely replied, "My commander heard that this was a children's home and sent me to bring some stuff for you. So if you will allow me, my men would like to unload it wherever would be convenient for you."

When he opened the truck for me to see, it was completely filled with food. Out of the blue, his commander had sent a truck full of food in the very hour that we ran out of food. I saw that day that God answers prayer! I estimated that the truck held enough food for three full months. As I fought back the tears, I asked if the men would wait a little longer to unload it until the boys got home from school. I wanted to make sure my kids did not think that their Dad had pulled strings to get this food, but that they would see that God was the one who provided.

Chapter 2 – Experiencing God in My Ignorance

The men shut the doors of the truck and we waited. When the boys came into the courtyard, they looked with curiosity at the truck. One of the younger boys asked, "Dad, did you buy this new truck?"

I wanted to laugh, "How could we possibly buy a new truck when we don't have money for food?"

I lined the kids up and asked them in front of the officers, "Kids, what were you praying for?"

One of the boys, Ajay, seven years old, was so excited, "Dad, I was praying for Hot Wheels!"

"What else were you praying for?"

"Dad, we were praying for food."

All the boys answered as well, "We were praying that God would provide."

As the men opened the doors to the truck, I told them, "God heard your prayer." God delights in the prayers of his children.

The boys saw all the food, which included cookies and other snacks; what luxuries! They all started crying and hugging me.

Later that day, I called up the commander that had sent the food to thank him. As I introduced myself on the phone, I said, "Sir I don't know you, but I'm really thankful for what you have done."

He explained to me that he and his wife had not been able to have children. "Last night," the man told me, "my wife could not sleep. She had heard that there was a children's center here and insisted that we send food to help the orphans."

I was speechless. That was exactly the same time that the orphans had been praying for food.

Chapter 2 – Experiencing God in My Ignorance

By God's grace, that food lasted for three full months.

The God Who Cares for His Own

A few weeks after this, I was in my office in the evening and heard a quiet knock on the door. I opened it and saw one of my boys, Bheem, standing there crying. Bheem was ten years old and had lost his vision a few years ago because of an infection. I invited him into my office and asked why he was crying. He responded, "Dad, whenever you give us homework, like to memorize a verse of Scripture, I can only do this by hearing the other boys memorize. It is so difficult for me because I cannot read the Bible for myself. I just have one desire, I don't desire to see anything else, my desire is to be able to read God's Word to be able to remember it."

Bheem's simple words struck my heart. His pure heart desired to read God's Word and yet, so many Christians have perfect vision but do not feel like reading God's Word.

I prayed for Bheem and made plans to see if anything could be done for him.

The next day, I took Bheem to get checked out at the hospital. Bheem was so excited that he was running into pillars and walls in the hospital. His brain could only hope that his vision was going to be returned to him that day. As he slammed against a pillar, because he could not see where he was going, he exclaimed, "I'm fine! I'm going to see, so it's never mind!" Before we left the hospital, I had to carry him on my shoulder to keep him from hurting himself by hitting anything else.

Chapter 2 – Experiencing God in My Ignorance

At the consultation, I learned that Bheem could have a surgery that would restore his sight. I was thrilled! Then the doctor told me how much that surgery would cost. The amount charged for the procedure was beyond my understanding. I thanked the doctor and walked home quietly. It hurt me inside because I had let Bheem get his hopes up. I wanted Bheem to be able to see more than anything, but I had no concept of where I would get that kind of money.

A few weeks later, a group of youth donated cricket balls, paddles, and other sports equipment to the orphanage. When they dropped off the new equipment, the youth challenged the boys to a cricket game. After a while, one of the leaders, a young man named Satish, approached me. He said, "I was pitching a ball to one kid, and for some reason wherever the ball was pitched, he missed it every time. He was swinging the bat in the air every time, but missing it completely… I felt bad, does this boy have some issue?"

I smiled because I knew Bheem liked to play cricket even though he could not see the ball being pitched. "That must be Bheem. He cannot see because his eyes were damaged from an infection."

Satish nodded and thought for a moment. He walked out of my office and dialed a number on his phone. Since he was standing in the hallway, I could hear parts of the conversation. He started talking to his Dad and explained about Bheem.

After a while, Satish came back into my office and sat down. He informed me that his Dad and he wanted to take care of Bheem.

"What do you mean?" I asked.

Chapter 2 – Experiencing God in My Ignorance

"Whatever the medical bill will be to make him be able to see again, we will pay it completely." I had not mentioned the surgery at all to Satish and yet he was going to completely pay for it.

As I listened to him, goosebumps covered my body. God was providing the money for Bheem's surgery. Think of it, a kid who desired nothing but to read God's Word was now going to get that chance!

Satish and his father donated the money and we scheduled the appointment for Bheem. Before the surgery was completed, I was invited to come to seminary in the United States. While directing the orphanage, I realized I needed to learn how to better counsel the orphans that I was taking care of. They were from hard places and I did not have the Biblical training I needed to help them. My uncle asked my brother to direct the orphanage in my absence. A few months into my studies, my brother sent me a video of Bheem with his Bible in his lap, reading, with his own eyes, Psalm 23, "The Lord is my Shepherd, I shall not want. . . ."

I grew up not wanting to associate with the God of the Bible, but He showed me over and over again His love for His children. The great Shepherd proved to me that He cares for His people. I have decided that I will serve the Lord for the rest of my life.

As I study now in seminary, my dream is to go back to India to start a Biblical counseling school. I desire to train the orphan students to counsel Biblically to go back to their villages and use God's Word to transform their communities.

Chapter 2 – Experiencing God in My Ignorance

About the Author – Nathaniel Thomas Varghese

Nathaniel Thomas Varghese is a Ph.D. student at Southwestern Baptist Theological Seminary in Fort Worth, Texas. He graduated with his Master of Arts in Biblical Counseling at Southwestern in 2018 and Bachelor of Arts in Business Management and Bible at Crossland College and India Theological Seminary in 2010. After serving in the banking sector for five years, God called Nathaniel to start an orphanage with Hopegivers International. Nathaniel's grandfather: Lt. Dr. M. A. Thomas, founded Hopegivers International in 1960 to reach orphans and pastors in India and train them to return to their villages as ministers of the word. Hopegivers International has trained more than 100,000 orphans over the years to go out and reach their community with the Gospel message. Hopegivers International works globally in rescuing the orphaned and abandoned in the society. If God has placed on your heart a desire to invest in the lives of these future ambassadors of the Gospel, please consider joining hands with us in training these children.

Chapter 2 – Experiencing God in My Ignorance

Hopegivers International
7300 Old Moon Road
Columbus, GA 31909
706-323-4673
Hopegivers.org

Nathaniel Thomas Varghese
Email: neelforchrist@gmail.com

Chapter 3

God Was There
By Rusti Weaver

I remember when I was a little girl, I would lie in bed, awake at night. Terrified, my mind racing, I can easily recall my fears overwhelming me... I felt as though they could swallow me alive.

It is now clear to me that was simply anxiety. I was learning the world's view of death, the finality of it, and the notion that one small twist of fate could be the end of everything you ever tried to accomplish. I was a preteen girl who became plagued with the thoughts of a life short-lived. So, I would lay there, and begin begging God to spare me of these horrible fates.

Quite simply, I was terrified.

I was young, but I understood I would be guaranteed a frightful fate if I dared to go wake my parents at 2 a.m. to tell them I was scared of the odd chance of developing cancer, being in a horrific car wreck, or becoming completely bedridden with an illness that would drastically change my life. After all, I was healthy, thriving, and had no need to fear

Chapter 3 – God Was There

something so rare and obscure. In turn, I did the only thing I knew was safe… I prayed, and God was there.

I finally grew out of that. Thank God, that anxiety and gnawing fear no longer crept in on me during the dark of night.

I excelled in school and socially. I met the most amazing man and got married. Just a few months after we wed, we took a risk greater than any other (reformed and self-diagnosed) hypochondriac could take…

We had children.

Babies! Oh, I was completely enamored. Why wouldn't you be? But oh, how you worry. As a parent, you literally section out a piece of your own heart and let it wander around in the world. Left to its own self, it inevitably returns to you injured, broken, or damaged, and your job, as its creator, are to mend its broken-ness the best you can and send it back to the world again.

All of my babies are incredible; it is amazing how each of them has their own ingrown traits, these remarkable diversities that distinguish them from their siblings. We loved getting to know each of them so much that we felt no hesitancy in having as many as it took to get my girl. It just so happens she didn't come along until we had five boys. Kaleb is our firstborn, he came in 2006; then we had identical twins, Brody and Brayden 13 months later; Chance came in 2009, and despite the three years between him and the twins, my body still thought I had room for two babies, so he was the big boy of the bunch. Isaiah is our baby boy, born in

Chapter 3 – God Was There

2012. He is our firecracker, the one who pushes you to the brink of your sanity. I did everything I could to try for those tutus and bows, I sweet-talked Josh into a final attempt for a girl, but most importantly, I prayed that God would recognize that we were pretty worn out, and in 2015, Abigail was born into our loud and loving family. If you read that right and are now needing to count on your fingers… it is six kids. Six huge pieces of my heart wandering around this earth apart from my own body. It can be scary. It can be overwhelming. I'll bring in my supreme, illimitable, all-powerful, life-saver that every mom, dad, and human being needs … God. Yes, God was there.

My best friend and the only person who could never let me down: The Father, The Son, and The Holy Spirit. Each integral, each needed so desperately in my life. Each one infallible, and amen, glory to God, Hallelujah, have I relied HEAVILY on Him over the years.

Life went on, and we did our thing; we raised kids, worked hard, and kept grounded in our faith. Then, in early Summer of 2016, the day came when things suddenly shifted. We knew *something* was happening, we just didn't know what. God had told my husband to prepare ourselves, that something was coming. No other clues, just… get ready. So, we did the only thing we knew to do: we dove into the word. We memorized Scriptures, declared entire passages of the promise, and we claimed affirmations over our family daily. We prayed for protection and peace. We didn't know what curveball would be thrown at us. We were in the process of buying a new house and selling our previous home definitely had its challenges! We lived in a camper trailer for weeks as

Chapter 3 – God Was There

we finalized details on our new home and waited (and waited and waited) for all the paperwork to be finalized. We started another school year, summer wrapped up, and I quit my job as a nurse to re-enroll in college for an advanced degree in the field of nursing. Each one of these things was a challenge; roll them all together in the same 60-day time span and it became clear that we were encountering huge life changes. Could this be what God was preparing us for? We thought, maybe it was. After all, it was an exhausting time.

Just as we got settled into our new home, our family was hit with a stomach bug. (Brand new home, furniture, carpet? Great! Now everyone vomit!) It worked its way through all eight of us. For Chance, it lingered (revert back to list: boy #4), though he would get sick in the morning before school and as the day progressed he would regain his strength and energy. I'd be sure he was clear to go to school the next day, then as he sat to eat his breakfast, and he would vomit on the way to the car. I began to question if he had the ability to make himself vomit, I mean, his timing was impeccable! When Brody then complained of a sore throat, the possibility of strep throat entered my mind. My kids don't present with the typical symptoms of strep. They will get nauseous, headaches, a cough, and Brody gets a rash. Paired with the vomiting Chance had, I called to make the pair an appointment with the pediatrician. A quick strep swab would solve this dilemma.

The next day we made our way into the doctor's office. Swabs were done, and as she looked over Chance, she asked the usual questions. Eating like usual? No, actually, he wasn't. Sleeping well? ALL the time, I was having trouble waking

Chapter 3 – God Was There

him and keeping him up through the day. Rash? No. Anything else abnormal? Well, he does have a bruise on his shoulder… it seemed like a random place for a bruise, and when I asked him, he said Isaiah jumped on him while he was in bed a few nights ago, but it still seemed strange to me.

THAT was the first time the thought crept in… leukemia. That's a trademark symptom of leukemia, bruising.

She looked at the bruise and felt his abdomen. She made a comment about checking the size of his liver and spleen. Because of my nursing background, this comment triggered the possibility of mono. Mono leaves you fatigued with a reduced appetite. Never in my life had I been so hopeful for a diagnosis like mono. She decided to draw some blood, and a dear friend that I attended nursing school with came in to get the labs. Chance was so scared, but she did great and he settled quickly. The strep tests for both kids returned normal, so we would have to wait for the blood tests. It would be the next day before those were back.

That evening we were supposed to go to an amusement park with some extended family. Chance was adamant he wanted to go, and his doctor said he could go, but not ride any rides. She was concerned his platelet count was low and that's why he was bruising. We debated back and forth and decided we could go and just have Chance play in the foam ball pit, but that was as far as he could go with any activities. He was too weak to walk through the park, so I pushed all 98 pounds of him in his sister's stroller. He watched YouTube videos and laughed with his cousins. When it came time to play in the ball pit, he excitedly jumped out of the stroller. We sat on the

Chapter 3 – God Was There

edge of the play area with our family members and watched the kids enjoying themselves. We split a few giant cinnamon rolls, and as we sat, we noticed Chance sitting down on the opposite side of the play area. I walked over to him and he ran his hand up to his thick, brown curly hair and sighed. "I'm just not feeling that good, mom. Can we go home?"' I felt his forehead... no fever. "Of course, Buddy." While we rode home, I replayed the conversation my husband and I had on the way to the park. Josh had asked me how the doctor's appointment went and what I thought was wrong with Chance. I whispered lowly to him that my greatest fear would be if they told us Chance had leukemia. He asked me if his symptoms were similar and I told him yes. Everything I saw him exhibiting did point to a possible diagnosis of leukemia. Of course, we hoped for a different explanation; I told my husband it could also be mono, or something viral...

But the next day would reveal just what kind of battle we would be thrown into. I called the office for results and was told the nurse would call me back very soon. Just a few minutes later my phone rang. I remember everything about that moment. I remember what I was wearing, exactly where I was sitting, how my house smelled... everything. The nurse told us to bring Chance in immediately. He would be admitted and likely be in the hospital for a few days at minimum. A blood transfusion was needed right away, but he would likely need much more work done. I sat down and inhaled a shallow breathe and spoke into my phone, "I know the rules regarding this, but I'm going to ask you anyway... are you going to tell me Chance has Leukemia?" As the words fell from my mouth, they sank into my stomach. "I

Chapter 3 – God Was There

can't answer that question, Rusti. Just bring Chance and Josh, and possibly another family member if you can. We will give you all the information we can when you get here."

I dropped my phone and ran. I ran past my kids' rooms where they were sleeping, outside and across the yard, barefoot. Not a shred of thought passed through me that I neglected to put on shoes. It was now November, and the ground was cold and wet. I needed out and away. I ran to my sister-in-law, Tisha's house next door. I pounded and knocked and glanced down at my feet. Pieces of leaves clung to my skin and dew soaked them. I pulled my sweater close and crossed my arms while I waited for her to answer. She peered out and could read my fear all over my face. She stepped out to meet me on her front porch asking what had happened.

"It's bad," I told her. "They got Chance's blood tests back and they need us to bring him in to the hospital. They said he needs to be admitted, and at least have a blood transfusion; he needs it right away. They told us to bring in family members with us… I know what that means, they are going to tell us something bad!"

Tears were now rolling for both of us. Refusing to allow it though, she shook off the words I just said. "No! Rusti, we won't have ANY of this! We refuse to accept anything bad they try to speak over him! We know God has a plan for him and we know how to pray for him. He will be fine. He will be FINE."

I nodded in agreement, still in shock and disbelief of everything that was happening. At some point, I had called

Chapter 3 – God Was There

Josh and he pulled into the driveway as I crossed back through the yard to our house. He had been crying, "What's going on, what do we need to do now?" I told him we needed to get Chance ready to go to the hospital and to tell the kids what we know is going on, and to PRAY. I knew in the back of my mind what was about to happen. I knew what it meant when doctors tell you to bring family into the results appointment with you. I have been the nurse on the other end of the phone call, saying I couldn't give any more information. It meant we were about to give life-changing news. It meant the news would be so difficult to grasp that we would need more than one set of ears there so that if bits of information got lost on one person, the other might be able to soak it in. I just knew.

We came back into the house and I woke up Chance to tell him the doctor needed us back up at the hospital and we were leaving now. Josh told the other boys to get dressed and get ready to go to Tisha's house. I hurried and got dressed and brushed my teeth. Josh came in, but neither of us spoke a word. As we walked back into the living room, Chance came out of the room. "Can you help me get dressed?" I grabbed a set of clothes and slid them on for him and he sat down on the couch. I stepped back and took him in… my sweet boy, chubby, rosy cheeks, just beautiful. I loved him so much, he was my heart. He sat there, head down, shaking. He was so scared. *How do we do this, God?* We hadn't a clue. When the other kids were all dressed we stood in a circle around Chance, we all laid hands on him and prayed for him. Everyone cried. No one understood what was going on or what our future held. The kids went to their Aunt's, and we

Chapter 3 – God Was There

loaded up in the car with Chance and Josh's mom and headed to the pediatrician's office.

They ushered us right away to a room. As we passed through the halls, we saw Doctor Caroline opening the door to an exam room. She was our pediatrician and a longtime family friend, someone we attended church with for many years, and we trusted her with our babies. She caught our stare in the hall, closed the door behind her, and passed the chart to another nurse, "I'm going over to the hospital with them. If this patient doesn't want to wait, reschedule them." Chance hopped up on the table and we stood around him. Caroline came in with her nurse with a stack of lab results in her hands. She held them out to me, "Um, it looks like leukemia." She said, "With his counts as high as they are, I don't know what else it could be. My only assumption would be leukemia." Instantly, all the air seemed to be sucked out of the room. My mind seemed to shut off.

I heard Josh softly whimper, "No," in a voice I'd never heard from him before. My hand instinctively reached over to Chance... he sat on the exam table, completely unaware of what was happening around him. As I touched his leg I felt something move in my spirit; God was there. He reminded me of when I was pregnant with Chance. At the end of my pregnancy with him, the doctors were afraid something wasn't right. They ordered extra tests and made me see a specialist. During that time, we were all praying. We called all our extended family who were believers and asked them to pray for health for our baby. On the day we had been to the specialist, we were waiting for results from the tests when Josh's mom called in tears. She told us grandma was praying

Chapter 3 – God Was There

for the baby and heard the voice of God, loud and clear. It said to her, "This child will be a mighty man of God, and the name they are looking for… is Aaron." Grandma didn't know we had been searching for a bible name for his middle name. She hadn't any idea we didn't have his whole name already picked out, but that settled it. Our baby would be fine, and his name was to be Aaron. We rejoiced in God's presence and His promise. The doctors confirmed later that same day that everything looked great and they were no longer concerned.

So how did we get here? Seven years later in a different doctor's office and they were telling me my child had leukemia? The possibility, the earth-shattering reality completely escaped me, but God was there. He reminded me of exactly what my heart needed in that very moment. He said, "Aaron WILL BE a mighty MAN of God… he is not a man yet."

That's right! He is NOT a man yet! He is only seven! God didn't tell us he would be a mighty *child* of God, He knew he would be a man. His story doesn't stop here! It can't!

My heart rate instantly slowed, and it was as though the Holy Spirit squared my shoulders and straightened my posture. I was brought back to the present situation with an encouragement of "You got this… GOD'S got this." The burden was taken, just as fast as it was given. God gave me the best gift in that moment. *Peace.*

I could have easily refused to accept it. Instead, I said "Yes, God. I choose *your way.*"

Chapter 3 – God Was There

Just seconds before, my greatest fear in the entire universe was realized. Only it wasn't me… it was my child. My baby. God moved though, and gave me the courage to say, "Let's do this."

I can attest to the fact that my reaction was NOT my own. My body, my strength, my soul, *everything* in me was shattered. I felt as though I could have crumpled into a shapeless heap on the cold white tile of that room. If it was just me, I would have faltered.

We made a *choice,* we accepted that HE would sustain us, we accepted that HE was our strength, we accepted that HE was our healer. Not a day went by where Chance didn't believe without a doubt that he would be okay and this would all soon be a part of our story. This was his story, he knew it was for him to share and help others. He stepped into the shoes that God gave him to fill, and he filled them to overflowing.

Now, to the outside world it was obvious we were faced with a huge battle. Did we have peace? Yes. Did we have comfort from the Holy Spirit? Oh yeah. Did we know that Chance would be healed? Absolutely.

Were there times when we were weak? Without a doubt. Yes.

We are not perfect, we didn't get through this war without scars.

When Chance arrived at St. Jude and we received the official diagnosis of Acute Myeloid Leukemia, we were still in shock, our whole world shifted. We were ripped from our life and

Chapter 3 – God Was There

transferred into a nightmare. The day we got there, we were told they would be placing a port in Chances chest and he would begin a low chemo dose immediately to get his white cell count down due to the fact that it was dangerously high. He was at risk of developing blood clots in his lungs. As they wheeled him down to surgery for the port placement, I was walking alongside the stretcher, holding his hand, and he looked up at me with tears streaming down his cheeks and said, "This is really serious, isn't it?" The gut-wrenching reality of it had hit him and hit me, too. All I could do was squeeze his hand and whisper, "You are going to be fine, buddy."

They allowed me to stay in the OR until he was asleep. I watched his eyes slowly close and the surgical team swung into action. This was their everyday job, but for us, it was anything but normal.

As I walked out of the OR, the reality hit me like a brick wall. It was as though the words, tests, and protocols they had been explaining to us all formed together into a giant wrecking ball that suddenly collided with my understanding. I had to accept the fact that while he was under anesthesia, Chance would receive his first chemo.

Chemo.

My baby… is getting *chemo*.

A nurse met me outside the OR doors, and as it all struck me, I collapsed into her arms. I'd never met her, but it was like she just knew. She held me and allowed me to sob into her hair. In that moment, I was alone and safe. Safe to be the

Chapter 3 – God Was There

vulnerable mom who was terribly heartbroken for her child. I was free to be the wife who had no clue how to keep her husband strong. In that moment, I didn't have to be strong for anyone and I allowed myself to be broken. We all need that too. Ecclesiastes chapter 3 tells us there *IS* a time to break down, weep, mourn, and *this was my time*.

Chance came out of surgery like a champ. He took on those first low doses of chemo extremely well, so much so that there were times he would be actively getting an infusion and he'd decide to go play with his brothers in a different room on the floor. We would get him out of bed, I would unplug his IV pump from the wall, and we'd arrange the three or four lines all running into his port in my hand. Then he would take off! Once he was going so fast down the hall, I had the sense of what the owner of a St. Bernard must feel like when they take them for walks. I would constantly urge him, "Slow down, Bud!" as I tried to keep all the lines free from being trampled or caught in the wheels of the IV stand. One day we just happened to pass by a teenage girl walking with her mom down the same hall. Except her mom wasn't holding onto her daughter's lines, or being dragged along. Instead, she was gripping a gait belt that was wrapped around her daughter's waist to keep her upright. The girl's face winced in pain with each step she took. She was bald, pale, and beautiful. As we passed them my heart ached and I glanced back in front of me to see my son's head (at that time, still full of hair) barreling down the hall, and I sent a silent praise to God for Chance's strength and energy. I didn't tell him to slow down. Instead, I let him run.

Chapter 3 – God Was There

It wasn't long after we arrived at St. Jude that Chance decided to have the staff call him Aaron. When the staff introduced themselves on each admission, they would ask him if he went by Chance or another name/nickname. One day he said, "I want you to call me Aaron, it's my middle name." To us, this was a much-welcomed confirmation! Aaron didn't know I was standing on that promise. He had no clue that word from God was my foundation I leaned into each day when I felt weak. He made that decision on his own, and to us, it was God's way of showing us THIS is his testimony. THIS is what I will use to open the door for others to be blessed by this boy's faith.

Before Aaron got sick (and during), I was in a MAJOR 'dry spell' with God. Have you ever had those times where you are BEGGING, PLEADING, and doing everything in your power to make God move… and… crickets… Yeah. I was there. It had been YEARS since I'd had a big God revelation and I was really down about it. I was so incredibly hungry for more of the Holy Spirit, but couldn't cross that steep, empty, hollow divide.

Please hear me when I say this: God is GOOD. I will never say He is a God who holds back to be distant or mean. He needs us EQUIPPED for the battles we face. God needed my faith to be unshakeable. Aaron got sick and I had faith. The Spirit of God was with us, no doubt… Did I experience the Holy Spirit in an audible way? Nope. But the second he was diagnosed, God was there. He instantly reminded me of the promise he gave us when Aaron was still in my womb! Day in and day out. With every hospital admission, chemo treatment, those long days and weeks away from my other

Chapter 3 – God Was There

babies, I stood. Unwilling to move. THAT is where God needed me. If He had been constantly talking me through the simple (in comparison) trials of life beforehand, I can tell you, I would not have ever been able to be strong enough to withstand a battle like this one. I would have relied on God to take it away immediately instead of leaning on what I already knew. Our faith isn't only to be used in the beginning of trials when we don't understand, or at the end when our strength feels completely depleted. It comes into play in the *middle*. We need it most when we are deep in the dark crevice of the valley, where we look back and see what we have encountered and then look ahead and see the long path back up to the daylight. THAT is where an immovable faith comes into active play. It means we DON'T LOSE HOPE. We know what promises to cling to, we know where our help is! (Yes! Even when He is silent!)

What I hope to encourage you to do as God's precious child is to simply NOT let the storms of life enter your hearts. Our job is to access and dwell in the peace of God. I know at times it seems an impossible task, but I want you to consider this. We can be completely innocent (consider Job) and still endure really tough trials. I am talking, REALLY tough. That is when the peace of God comes into play. This gift that God freely gives us is already at our fingertips! It already belongs to us! It is IN our possession! God sent his Holy Spirit to be with us, he promised that He would NEVER leave us, and when we accepted Christ as our LORD, that means we obtained the Holy Spirit to live with us forever! God is there.

We *will* encounter trials, God himself says this in his Word. (John 16:33) Not IF, but WHEN we encounter trials, He will

Chapter 3 – God Was There

be with us. He will shoulder the burden, He will renew us, refresh us, restore us. *He* tells us this. Do you believe God is a liar? NO! But the devil is! The devil will try to convince you to take on the battle on your own, he will distract you, he will scare you, and leave you feeling powerless. In Romans 8:37, God says we are MORE than conquerors. I fear that people tend to just spout the last few words of that Scripture without accepting those last few words are where the power lies: ***THROUGH CHRIST JESUS***. He is our gift! He will take on any fight, illness, and fear that you may have and conquer it for you. Your requirement is to press into that power, you have to surrender it to him! That is the only way to enjoy life through the storm.

Let me pose this question to you: when you think of sleep, how does it make you feel? I am talking the nice, deep, peaceful sleep where you wake up feeling completely rejuvenated and strengthened. (The kind you very well may be missing out on and have for some time!)

Does it make you happy? Smile? Do you crave it? Do you long for that kind of rest and refreshing? In Mark chapter 4 it speaks of a terrible storm hitting the ship that Jesus and his disciples were on as they were crossing the sea of Galilee. This was not your run-of-the-mill thunderstorm, this was what the Bible called a "furious storm." The boat was lashing about, waves were crashing over the edges flooding the boat, and his disciples gathered to figure out what they needed to do. When they got together, they noticed one integral piece of their group wasn't there: Jesus! Where was he? He was sound asleep! His disciples were absolutely bewildered that

Chapter 3 – God Was There

he was peacefully sleeping in the midst of that furious storm. They had to shake him awake and ask him to calm it!

Jesus wasn't sitting up in the dark corner of the cabin nauseated from the waves, He wasn't laying there, waiting for His father to stop the ferocious sea; he was dead asleep.

I imagine them waking Him much like how my kids do in the middle of the night: "Mom! I'm scared, I saw/heard/this or that, and now I am too afraid to rest!!!" When I picture this scenario, I see Jesus reluctantly swing his legs over the edge of his pallet as he pulls himself upright. He yawns, stretches, and trudges half asleep behind his scared children to the deck of the boat. He examines the situation, yep, nothing He can't handle. He speaks to the sea and tells it to calm down and hush, he pats his kids on the head and turns around to go back to bed.

That's it! The God of the UNIVERSE, the creator of the heavens, can place the stars in the sky, but you think your debt/illness/whatever it may be is TOO much for him?! He told the oceans where to stop, but you refuse to lay your burdens at His feet? Why would we ever do that to ourselves?

It's time to tap into that peace and joy. It's time to let it overwhelm you. We need to allow ourselves to dwell in it, soak it in, and let it absolutely SATURATE us! That way when life happens, when we incur that trial, that burden, we are just dripping with Jesus. God is here, and if you allow him to, that peace and joy can follow you wherever you go.

Chapter 3 – God Was There

Chance Aaron completed his treatment and was able to come home April 1st, 2017. He achieved remission after his first round of chemo in December. Doctors told us to expect to be at St. Jude for a minimum of 6 months, more than likely 8 months. We were there a total of 4 and a half months. The entire time we were there we believed for supernatural healing, the kind that would make him stand out so that we could share God's goodness with those who asked. We were able to do just that. He was asked to do a photo shoot for the hospital and be used in their advertising campaigns. After a year of clear bone marrow biopsy's in March of 2018, Aaron was recognized as CURED by his oncologists. (We claimed, believed, and spoke that he was cured from the beginning.) Proverbs 18:21 says that there is the power of life and death in our tongues and we were determined to use every weapon we were equipped with. His life, his testimony, is a gift. Opportunities to share his story continue to present themselves and we jump on them! As his 9th birthday is fast approaching, we look forward to celebrating all that God has gifted us with. We had our season of sorrow. We endured our season of hardship and we allowed God to mold us through the trials. Watching Aaron battle leukemia was incredibly difficult for our entire family, no doubt. Now we have the honor of entering into our season of joy. A part of me will always believe that our harvest of joy began in the midst of the sorrow. It was all because of the burden that we were able to delight in the small victories. The daily belly laughs from Aaron, watching him demolish a plate of bacon cheddar fries after days of nausea, seeing his cheese sauce mustaches were a sight for sore eyes. Philippians 4:8 encouraged us to focus on THE GOOD in our

Chapter 3 – God Was There

circumstances. Look around, God is there, and because of Him... there is so much GOOD.

About the Author – Rusti Weaver

Rusti is from a small town in central Missouri. She holds the title of wife to Josh, mom to six, former working nurse, and current crazed homeschooling mom. Her background in healthcare became a tremendous benefit after her fourth son, Chance Aaron, was diagnosed with Acute Myeloid Leukemia in late 2016. As a way of healing and keeping family back home updated she began a Facebook journal documenting their venture into the world of pediatric cancer. Overwhelmed by the support of her community, the page quickly became an avenue for her to pour out her heart, sharing the ups and downs of all they encountered. Writing also provided the confirmation she needed to begin the active pursuit of becoming a professional author. As their story unfolded, many were moved by the joy and peace God was able to provide them during the most heartbreaking of circumstances. By His grace and {not so} gentle nudges, Rusti is now putting His goodness to paper with the hopes of also branching out into public speaking. Her point of view is that God gave her a

Chapter 3 – God Was There

story to tell and she is going to tell it, even if it means doing it with shaky hands. Rusti finds joy in her quiet time with God, date nights with her husband of 13 years, a great beach vacation, and a good bag of salt 'n' vinegar potato chips. If you would like to read through Chance Aaron's journey go to: www.facebook.com/crushingitinfaithwithchanceaaron or you can contact Rusti directly at:
www.facebook.com/rusti.weaver

Chapter 4

On the Other End
By David Simon Reyes

Have you ever had that kind of mindset that every time the new year comes, you'll ask God what your next year is going to be like? Well, I don't know if that's weird for you, but God does answer those silly questions of mine. 2016 was a year of struggles for me; it was simply one of my darkest years. I struggled back and forth with depression and anxiety; my insecurities were all over me, and I was into all other vices. With a crawling and devastated soul, I asked God what's up for me in the next year. He simply told me, 2017 is where I'm going to grow. He will take me to heights and experiences I've never had or been before. Boy, He wasn't kidding. 2017 wasn't pleasant at all, but it was where I discovered my spiritual gifts. God gave me a ministry where His power inside of me was manifested mightily. All my talents and gifts were honed and used. I was brought to levels outside my comfort zone; I went to missions, conferences, concerts, divine retreats, and a whole lot more. So as 2017 ended, I talked to God and asked Him like a child asking questions to his dad, "God, it has been a rough ride. Do you have something big for me next year? I mean c'mon." He smiled at me and said, "2018 is going to be the year of

Chapter 4 – On the Other End

opportunities for you." I'm not going to lie, it made me feel so excited. I was all motivated and just pumped up for 2018 to start. But then He calmly told me after my celebration, "I'm going to take you to deeper waters." Honestly, I didn't know what He really meant at first until that season of my life came, where everything about me went downhill.

Have you ever had those moments with God where what He said isn't matching up with what He's doing? Like let's be real, He promised me a year of opportunities, but 2018 came, and it's where I lost my job on a very bad note. It was where I drowned in anxiety and depression again. It was where I experienced and saw how real spiritual warfare was. Life was torturing me in all aspects. From my finances, my spiritual life, my family, ministry, and my relationships, I lost myself and had forgotten who I was. There were times I would go up to the rooftop of a building and just pray my heart out to God up there, crying and just being real with Him. I was asking where He was, I was reminding Him of His promise; I was confessing my doubts and fears to Him. Doesn't that sound familiar to most of us? In this story of mine, I'll be discussing the three characteristics of God which I've gotten to know throughout my journey.

The God of All Seasons

I honestly thought at first that in this world, when you do good things and work hard along 'the system', you'd be successful. I was naïve and thought that life would eventually be fair. As it is said in the Scriptures, what you reap is what you sow (Galatians 6:7), so I kind of adopted the same approach to my faith in my early years. It seemed to sound

Chapter 4 – On the Other End

right and accurate. But I didn't dig deeper into the whole picture of its context, which led me to a performance-based identity.

I can still remember those days in my youth, I was already a known God-fearing man in our university's ecosystem or community. Many females admired me for it, hence, it became sort of a unique selling proposition for me. But what most people didn't know was that I was only building a shiny façade where I could hide my struggles over its shadows. I was struggling during those times with depression, which made me resort to casual sex for comfort. God gave me a platform and whether I admit it or not, I knew I was one of the popular guys on the campus. I had that Mr. Godly Gentleman Mysterious guy branding, which gave me the confidence to do such reckless acts. I was implicitly using God for my own selfish desires when it should've been the other way around. Every time I committed a sin of any various type, I tried to make it up to God by creating another Christ-centered blog post that I would share on my social media. There was even a point where I felt numb even after realizing the mistakes I had done. I couldn't feel the Holy Spirit's convictions anymore. There was a time where I was convinced that I was already spiritually dead. I would go into my dormitory room and lock myself there. I felt empty. I felt like I was drenched in the dark, even when my day totally went well. To be honest, even now as I'm trying to remember these moments of my life for this project, I'm beginning to be teary-eyed.

For the most part in my university days, I normally just woke up, went to school, went to work, then went to a computer

Chapter 4 – On the Other End

library to work my thesis there by myself, went home to rest for two hours, and back at it again. It was that routine for me. I withheld myself away from any godly community. I stopped attending church services, refrained from talking to my godly friends, pretended that I was alright to other people like my 'bros' and my colleagues, talked to God only when I felt like it – I was living life like I was just waiting for it to end. One may ask, what did I do for leisure back then? As bad as it may sound, I simply talked to women with the hopes to find satisfaction as I tried to earn their trust and admiration. I was a very insecure guy and the approval of other people had become the source of my reassurance that I was still "good".

It went on and on for almost a year until nothing that this world gave me was enough to give comfort for the dreading depression that was slowly eating me alive. I was already having those days where I would go mad and just cry for no reason at all. I was having trouble sleeping, even when my body was already dead tired; it felt like something was after me, so I had to stay awake. I was restless. My vices weren't enough to comfort me. I tried socializing and going out with other people despite my tight schedule in hopes to find my 'calm pill'. I always came home, tired, empty, and just plain suicidal. I was screaming inside my room alone, I was punching my wooden cabinet, and punching myself. As crazy as it may sound, feeling physical pain was more appealing to me than trying to make it through another anxiety attack brought about by my depression. That was, as I call it, an 'abstract agony'.

Chapter 4 – On the Other End

I knew I had to stop pretending that I could keep on going with this lifestyle. For several weeks, I cried out to God in solidarity, asking for His forgiveness and His comfort to fill me up again. I was bowing down to Him every time, and was just confessing every single pain, hurt, and struggle that I've had.

Eventually, I went back to church again. I knew it was the only place I could always go to, but it was just my ego and shame that was holding me back. It was so surreal. I was already crying because of my guilt while I was on the way there. The service hadn't even started yet, and my face was just in total tears. It was a habit of mine to stay in the dark corner of the church hall while the music session was ongoing. I didn't want anyone to see me crying. I wrestled with myself to keep my poise or to keep myself together, but who was I kidding? In front of the Almighty, inside His presence, we can never hide anything from Him. It's all out there exposed. All I could ever do during that time was cry in total repentance. After spending several youth services in that church near my dormitory, a campus minister messaged me on Facebook and asked me if we could have some coffee. I agreed, though it was strange because both of us never knew that we were already friends on Facebook until he chatted with me. Long story short, he introduced me to his small group and to the church staff. I knew it was God who was moving. God gave me a godly circle of friends again, not only for me to learn from them, but for me to also share the wisdom He had given me.

One thing I can never forget was when we talked about "isolation." I never knew that putting ourselves in isolation

Chapter 4 – On the Other End

was one of the enemy's actual strategies to finish us off. Whenever I was hurting or had committed something shameful, I always kept it to myself. I was afraid someone would judge me, that I could never be understood, that I would be condemned, that someone would blackmail me – I had every logical reason to stay 'quiet' about my internal battles. What I didn't know was that the enemy can attack us more effectively when we're alone. I didn't have a godly circle back then, not even a mentor, nor anyone I could look up to. But when I prayed to God in total repentance and surrendered, He was the one who already made a way for me to have everything that I needed to fight back. If you're struggling with depression just like me, staying in isolation can be a deadly decision. Talk to God and be open to Him. Out of everyone, it's imperatively impossible for God to not understand someone He has created. Dude or Dudette, I can assure you that even before you speak, He already knows what you're exactly feeling (Matthew 6:8). All you have to do is to 'come' as you are, not who you ought to be. One of the reasons I see why Jesus had to come down here on this wretched world and experience the climax of pain it could ever give was so that He could remind us that whatever we're going through, whatever we're feeling – He understands it fully (Hebrews 4:15-16). He's gone through it. He knew what it's like to be tempted, rejected, betrayed; He knew what it was like to be thirsty, to be bullied, unappreciated, and scorned.

When I graduated, I went immediately to work full-time in the corporate world. Because of my interpersonal skills, I landed a job in the field of sales. At first, I was excited, even

Chapter 4 – On the Other End

though it was very irrelevant from the degree I earned, and it was very new to me. I thought I would eventually learn to love it and excel in the industry. I guess I was wrong, and I learned it the hard way. Almost a year passed by and I was still the least performing employee in our roster. Don't get me wrong, I was really trying. I was studying the products and our clients, I was acquiring online lessons for my job - I was doing pretty much all I could. Though, to be honest, I was very blessed still. My bosses were so kind to me that they treated me like a little brother or a son that was just lost in his career pursuit. My company was great, my compensation was too, but I couldn't bear to fail them over and over again.

From being an achiever, I felt like a dumb dude at my work. I dreaded every morning, knowing I had to do something I sucked at. I told myself to keep on going, that this was just a phase of my life I had to go through. Failing was something not new to me, but having other people, my team, affected because of my incompetence in the job was something I deeply condemned myself about.

During those times, I was asking God why He would put me in a place or a position where I would fail? Where is His promise? Where is the year of opportunities He was talking to me about? I was mad at God for some time. I knew it was God who gave me that job and my place in the business district of Metro Manila, but it made me wonder why I was consistently failing and why my debt in the bank was only getting larger. I knew I have my faults, but I was asking God for help. Where was He?

Chapter 4 – On the Other End

But as time went by, I began to realize that the more important question for me to ask was not *where* He is. He can never get lost, but rather to ask myself, *who* He is? Who is God to me in my times of failures, distress, and trials? Is God only good when my life is good? Is His goodness only dependent on my life's circumstance or situation? Those were the questions I started pondering.

God was trying to teach me something. I was asking God where He was, but then He replied back and asked me where my faith was. He was trying to tell me that His identity is constant. He is never-changing. Though our circumstance may change, His love, mercy, and grace never does. He began to ask me questions, "When you were in your dark seasons, did I ask you where you were? Did I stop loving you? When you left, have I forgotten who you are to Me?"

I guess we've all been in some point of life where our faith is forged into flames to verify its authenticity. God was building me, but He was also exposing me. He was putting me into deeper waters. He was trying to show me that who He was in my season of victory is the same as who He is regardless of whatever season I am in. He is my God, my fortress, my deliverer, my shield, my portion and my strength - even when my life is falling apart (Psalm 18:2).

As my season of failures continued, I noticed something. I started to meet directors, models, hosts, and other media-related people, and they were all curious about me. They all wanted to work with me in certain projects, but due to my corporate job's schedule, I couldn't. Ever since I was in high school, I was interested in making films. When I was in

Chapter 4 – On the Other End

college, I enjoyed working for student film productions as their host and actor. I knew that the entertainment industry was something I'd always wanted to pursue, but due to its unpredictable career stability, I opted to be safe and practical. After a period of time, I was faced with a life-changing moment. I had to choose between my corporate job and an open door for me to pursue my passion, which was modelling, acting, hosting, and the like. I told myself that I had a lot of monthly bills to pay and my bank debt was only getting larger by the moment. Choosing a not-so-stable career with an unpredictable monthly income was going to be a huge risk for me. But then I looked at my corporate job and I couldn't help but admit that I was so tired of it already. It was as if I was a working zombie every single morning. There was no joy, no sense of fulfillment, no passion, and no peace. I prayed to God about it tremendously. Then I figured, there is no way God wouldn't give me the skills and the love for this type of industry if it were for nothing. I told God, "Lord, if this is really Your will for me, I'm willing to face the risk, but please hold me. Don't let me fall, but when I do, please sustain me."

After that month, I resigned from my corporate job and pursued acting and modelling. Projects and different opportunities were coming to me left and right. My google calendar had never been so busy until then. That's when I realized that God had me go through all of those trials because He was preparing and building me. He humbled my character, He enabled me to know my strengths and weaknesses more, and He made me more dependent on Him. Before every series of blessing comes a process of testing. I would fail or get lost instantly in this industry if I wasn't able to grow and mature as an individual in both emotional and spiritual aspects.

Life might not be fair, but as the popular saying goes, "God is good ALL the time." His identity is not based on our ups and downs. He is who He is. He is my God in my failures and successes, in my victories and defeats, in my joy and my sorrows. God has loved me despite knowing all facets of who I am. He was faithful to me even in the times I was faithless to Him. Romans 5:8 says, "But God demonstrates his own love for us in this: While we were still sinners, Christ died for us." God blessed and cherished me even amid my drenching myself in my sins. He is with me when I'm at my best, and He is with me even at my worst. Therefore, He is the God of every season of my life - pleasant or not. This was my battle cry in the 'desert'. I want you to close your eyes, and declare this statement aloud, "He is the God of all seasons. He is holding me together, even when my world is falling apart."

The Humble Pursuer

One night, I was praying to Him, and He suddenly gave me a vision. He showed me that during those times I was crying out to Him in prayer, He was actually beside me – crying too. If you think it hurts to be a follower of Jesus Christ, you haven't even scratched the surface of pain yet. Don't forget that it hurts so much more for a father to see his child suffer. As the Scripture says, we are His child (Galatians 3:26). You are His daughter, you are His son, and every tear His children

Chapter 4 – On the Other End

cry out is precious to Him. He is close to the brokenhearted (Psalm 34:18). He knows every wound of your heart. He is just waiting for you to give it all to Him. Don't do what I did – I tried to figure out things all alone. I was pretending that I would be fine, that I could go through this. Don't believe those lies. There are some unpleasant things in this world that God allowed me to go through that only He could mend; only He can heal and restore. I've heard in one of the preachings in our church that God actually created a place in our hearts that only He can fulfill.

If God calls me by my name despite my sins and declares to me that I am His child, disregarding everything He knows about me, including the unpleasant ones, I don't think there is anything out there in this world that could ever make me in awe the same way He does. His love saved me and is continually saving me from depression.

Just to add to this, Francis Chan made an illustration about God's love in one of his video podcasts. He said to imagine your child, or perhaps imagine that you have a child, and whether it might be a daughter or a son, imagine him/her being crucified on the cross to save people who resent you; people who don't even have a hint of guilt for their mistakes, and might never even acknowledge your child's sacrifice. Would you allow your child to go? Most of us, if we're honest, couldn't even bear to imagine our child getting hurt, or more, being crucified. But God did. God went through all of that pain in His thought of you and me. God was filled with love and mercy for us that He chose to sacrifice His one and only begotten Son. That is how much He loves you.

Chapter 4 – On the Other End

There was a time in my life where I wandered away from God again. I got too stressed and busy at my corporate job. I was bombarded with responsibilities, disappointments, and frustrations all at the same time. But of course, every time I attend church, I pretended to be alright to most people. One Sunday, I got to spend some time with a sister in Christ and her kids. I noticed that her eldest, who was 15 years old, was showing signs of depression. As someone who's gone through depression and is still battling it, I knew what it looked like. I immediately talked to her mom about it. That's when her mom started breaking it down to me. I asked permission if I could talk to her child privately to figure out what's beneath those fake smiles that her daughter has. As a close family friend, she allowed me. I talked to the young girl and she began crying to me like I was her dad. I told her a brief story of my depression and that's when she started talking about hers. The next thing I knew, I was preaching God's love for her and every single word that came out of my mouth hit my heart, too. I guess that's what the Scripture meant in Hebrews 4:12 when it says that the word of God is sharper than a double-edged sword. Technically, I was preaching to her, but to be real, the Holy Spirit was preaching to me through myself. God used that situation for me to be used in that little girl's struggle, and for me to be reminded of His love. I can barely count how many times God has used me, even during my wandering. Once you encounter God and experience having a personal relationship with Him, it is true that you will never be the same again. God was using different circumstances to pursue his lost child, which can be you or me.

Chapter 4 – On the Other End

How could God, the most Holy of Holies, the King of all Kings, take His precious time in pursuit of a man like me? I still couldn't comprehend it. Therefore, I am all the more determined to share this good news with those people whom I once was being. The lost, the broken, the ignorant, the unloved - the world needs you and me out there to show them His love. Let's use our lives as God's instruments in His pursuit of His lost children.

The Source That Lasts

When I was in my university days, we experienced a ton of thesis work. I was juggling my school and my job back then. Having 27 units while working as much as 35 hours a week, I barely got rest. It was stressful; I didn't have time for myself, for my friends, for God, and not even for my family. To make things a lot harder, I was tasked by my professors to lead two research teams. One was about conducting a new study in the field of tourism while the other was creating a business plan out of scratch with a limited budget. I was bombarded with all these responsibilities. I was restless. Whenever I was at work, all I could think about was my schoolwork, and vice versa.

I tried to lead the team the best way I knew back then; doing everything on my own while my teammates carried on the mini tasks. I spearheaded our business plan. Though I would ask for their suggestions and opinions, I really didn't care. Like all leaders, I was faced with team members who had disagreements, occasions where all of our other courses were too demanding, and even times where both my team

Chapter 4 – On the Other End

members and I weren't meeting our deadlines. To make the long story short, after putting my heart out in both papers, after not sleeping for five days straight on some occasions, after giving it my all, we were only given a C+. I couldn't blame the panel though. Our presentation and the way our paper ended up didn't even pass my standards at all. I contemplated for some time, asking myself what happened. At first, I was thinking that it was my team members' fault for doing a lousy job in their delegated tasks, but still, those reasons weren't enough to give me a peace of mind. I certainly knew that there was something I failed to do. That's when it hit me. I didn't even include God in any of my plans. I did everything literally with my own strength and my own wisdom. I had people around me whom I could've maximized, but still, I was too full of myself. It was such a huge slap to my face. I prayed about our paper, yeah, but deep inside, I knew I didn't even have God in the process of making it.

Another semester came, and I was faced with another thesis course. I was assigned to lead a research team again. This time, I learned from my mistakes. When I first met my team members, I tried to get to know each one of them personally. I not only treated them like more than just co-researchers, but as real friends. I would have the team bond together and try to genuinely listen to their suggestions. This time, I submitted to the majority's decision after it had been hypothesized by each member of the team. As I got to know them more, I began to see how they could contribute to our paper. I tried to maximize their strengths and their weaknesses, and even tried to delegate the degree of

Chapter 4 – On the Other End

responsibilities equally. It was almost as if I was not even in the picture. But trust me, it was the best experience ever. It wasn't easy at all, though. I was leading a team of seven, of which three of them had internships, one of them was a varsity player, two had full units, and there's me, a working student. But then again, just like any research team, we had our disagreements and conflicts. I was handling people with very different personalities, most of which were dominant and high-tempered ones. But I was surprised that I was able to handle every issue well without siding with anyone whenever conflict arose. Every time someone highlighted the mistakes or shortcoming of another, God gave me the wisdom to focus on finding a solution instead of convicting my members. I always encouraged my team to just carry on and move forward and let me do the talking whenever one member fell short of his/her fulfillment. I always encouraged eating together and praying before and after every meeting. I knew for sure that God was with me.

After several months, judgement day came. Our paper ended up in the top five research papers in our whole institution. It was a breakthrough unlike any other. How could a team full of busy individuals manage to do such a feat? I was commended by my professors, and even the panelists were impressed with my team. I knew it was God. It was all Him who did everything.

This is just one of the countless occasions I've realized that without God in me, I am truly nothing. This was what St. Paul meant when he said he couldn't boast about anything (1 Corinthians 1:26-31). As I grew closer and more intimate

Chapter 4 – On the Other End

with God, people around me started noticing the maturity with which I talked and lived at my young age. My friends even joke around that I'm a man in my 20's who speaks like I'm in my 40's. To some, they view me as an annoying, killjoy, old-school fellow, but to others, I was just a highly-principled man. The closer I get to God, the better I automatically become.

Don't get me wrong, I am trying to live by His word every day, and still, at times, I fall short. But what makes everything different was all the worldly things that I loved doing before, which were going to clubs, having casual sex, and getting wasted, have become the things I don't like doing anymore. My desire for these activities faded away (Psalm 37:4). Cussing has become a big issue for me. Even my taste for music slowly changed. Catchy tunes and sick beats weren't enough for my liking, and lyrics started to matter to me. I thank God for Christian Acoustics, RnB, and Hip-Hop music, though. To encapsulate what I'm trying to say is, our goodness, us becoming better, is only a by-product of our relationship with Jesus. He is the true source of goodness, and as we drink from Him as our living water, we begin to slowly reflect God's heart to other people (John 4:14). We're beginning to be able to give grace to other people, to let go of our worries and fears, to be happy even in the midst of a storm, to speak of positively in spite of our losses, and even to forgive without an apology. Galatians 2:20 says, "It is no longer I who lives in me but Christ who lives in me." My own goodness is not mine but His. We become more like Jesus when we spend more time with Him than the world.

Chapter 4 – On the Other End

And the tricky part is, we become more like the world when we spend more time in it than with Him.

Whenever I hear people saying that they're going to change through their own willpower, right then and there I know that they are bound to fail or fall short. Yes, pain and circumstances of life change people - some for the better and some for the worst. But if you truly want to change and discover who you really are and who you were meant to become, you go back to the Maker.

I had a phone back then, which for some reason broke. The battery was draining lightning fast. I used it for two hours and poof, it was sleeping again. I thought that if I went to this brand's official repair center, it would take me days or weeks to get it fixed and would cost me an expensive bill. So what I did was look for alternatives. Here in the Philippines, we have what we call "mass-market repair centers," those gadget stalls you normally see in the streets, and other marketplaces. I had my phone serviced there and I got it back just an hour after, and of course, with a better-priced bill. After a week, I noticed my phone was overheating. Thinking it was normal, I ignored it for two weeks until its performance was really slow. So I went back to get it repaired again, and this time they replaced a chip; I wasn't sure what it was. But oh well, as long as it works right? So after several weeks, my phone began to stop charging. So there I was again, going back to those mass-market repair centers, one after another until I found myself in a premium repair center. They told me that there was no way I could get my phone repaired again. The result was a compilation of different

Chapter 4 – On the Other End

uncertified spare parts in my phone. This was when I started regretting my choices. If only I went to a certified repair center from the very start, then I wouldn't be obliged to get a new phone again. All of those contacts, photos, messages, and memories, gone in one snap. That experience of mine can be a metaphor for our tendency as human beings when we search for comfort, security, and strength.

Oftentimes, all of us, especially when we're broken, have that urge to look for someone to fulfill our longings. We look for people who are willing to be with us, listen to our hurts, and understand our pain. I'm not saying that it's wrong, but when we seek repair from other people, we're only headed to another cycle of brokenness. Just like the story of my phone, we should have the Maker as our first and main source of comfort and peace. I have friends, both males and females, who go into one relationship after another thinking that someone in this world will fulfill them someday. We all have been there. I tried to seek refuge in my vices and other sins. But whatever the world offered me was only temporary and did great damage in the end. Similar to how a credit card goes, "enjoy now, pay later."

Every time I counsel people, I always pray to God in silence that He would guide my words, making sure that they are Biblically inclined and that it would lead the person to God and not to anyone else, including myself. Sometimes, it becomes so surprising how words of wisdom suddenly come out of my mouth. There were instances where these advises that I speak of should be preached to me as well. I was convinced that it was God speaking through me because I

Chapter 4 – On the Other End

knew that these words that I told people didn't come from me or my own wisdom. As a matter of fact, these words also hit me a lot. I realize that sharing God's word to other people isn't only beneficial to the listeners, but also it reminds the speaker a lot more of how great God is. In Hebrews 4:12, God's word is said to be sharper than any doubled-edged sword. Maybe that's what it meant. The wisdom that comes from God isn't only for the one who seeks, but also for the one who speaks.

He is the real source of life. The scripture says in John 5:15 that Jesus is the vine and we are the branches. Only those people who draw from Him can only bear fruit. If you want to be whole, if you want to discover your purpose, if you want to be the person that you were meant to be, if you want peace, comfort and strength that lasts, go to Jesus. He came down here on Earth not just to be a part of your life, but He wants to be the center of it. I want to live a life similar to how King David did, where everything about me, in both my victories and my defeats, will magnify God and God alone. God wants to be your best friend and He wants to hear your heart. Oh, you think God can't handle your brutal honesty? Trust me, whatever you want to say or ask Him, He knows it already. He's just waiting for you to spend time with Him with no boundaries. If you read the Psalms of King David, you see an overview of what spending time with God should look like. There were times King David would complain to God and even make reports about his enemies to God similar to how a 5-year old kid would to his dad. But also notice that with every burst of emotions King David speaks to God, he acknowledges who God is in His life and begins

Chapter 4 – On the Other End

to preach the heart of the Father to himself all over again. God doesn't want who you could become, God wants you. All you need to do is to accept His invitation and come as you are – even at your worst. Remember how the prodigal son in the book of Luke came back? He was dirty, filthy; he was a total mess. He was barely recognizable, yet the father, even from far away, immediately ran towards him, not to punish him, but to cherish his son and celebrate his homecoming.

When I was finally repenting to God after drowning myself into an insane period of vices, depression, and worldliness, God said only three words to me that forever changed my life. I was bowing down to Him for the first time in a long time, boldly coming to Him with a crushed spirit and a devastated heart. I apologized to Him tremendously, confessing all my guilt and shame. I saw God look down on me and heard Him say, "Go back home." At first, I didn't understand Him, but as time went by, I tried figuring it out. I started going back home to my family as much as I could, I visited the place where I first encountered God, I went back to regularly attending church services, and so forth. One Sunday, I was simply chilling in one of the seats in the church and there was a group of young adults, like me, who were chilling around there, too. Deep inside, I knew that I had been longing for a ministry or a consistent group of brothers and sisters with whom I could really bond with. I told myself that if one of the men in that group looks at me, I'll go talk to him. Lo' and behold, one guy stood up, looked at me, waved his hand, and invited me to join them. That was the start of me joining the young professionals' ministry, hence

Chapter 4 – On the Other End

my rapid growth. After more than a year, I'm deeply privileged to be chosen as one of the leaders of the ministry.

Conclusion

I'm always worried about a false sense of humility. I often ask God to remove any wrong motives in me. We sometimes still have wrong intentions whether we're conscious of it or not. I don't want to become famous making God famous, I want to make God famous and inspire other people to do the same. If becoming popular is a by-product of it, then with all my heart, I'm asking God to please refrain me from becoming a swell-headed person or a proud man.

There were times where I was compelled so much by the Holy Spirit to pray such brave things. These were moments where I get real with God. I asked Him to break me, expose me, and to use me. I knew that there were things in life that I couldn't attain without God breaking my heart and exposing my true self. There are truly some lessons in life that you can only learn in tragedy. Therefore, with a sincere heart, I urge you to rejoice in every season of your life. Run to God and make Him your primary source of strength, wisdom, and comfort. He is just waiting for you to come back home. Look around you. I may not know what's going on in your life, but He is pursuing you. No matter where you've gone, just look up and you will see - He is on the other end.

Chapter 4 – On the Other End

About the Author – David Simon Reyes

A young dreamer and aspiring entrepreneur, aiming to be a world-renowned Christian motivational speaker, David Simon is a determined achiever and has been ever since he was in his high school days. Attaining a bachelor's degree in Tourism Management from Far Eastern University in Manila while working as a barista in Starbucks for two years, alongside leadership engagements in various student organizations, earning a civil service license, and having national certifications for events management and front office management, David has always been an eager learner. Starting an early career in the foodservice industry, he moved into the field of sales and marketing both in the IT and real estate industry. After spending some time in the corporate world, David Simon noticed that his passion for film and media never faded away. Despite his financial problems, he took the risk of pursuing his desired path. Today, he is a freelance film and theater actor, advertising model, events host, and an independent marketing consultant in the Philippines. With his personal brand gaining more exposure, he was invited to join the world of pageantry where he won the grand title of Mister Grand Philippines in the year of 2018. While continually working in the industry for several months, he was appointed to be the

Chapter 4 – On the Other End

executive director of a newly established talents and events management company called "Bella Vie." Throughout all these years, this young man has been battling depression and anxiety which made him backslide several times from his faith - but has also become the source of his testimony of how God's love never failed him. He is now a part of the leadership team that caters to a ministry for young professionals in one of the mega-churches in the Philippines, wherein he also gets invited to speak to youth camps of different organizations. He now seeks to help more people simply by becoming the man God wants him to be in every platform he's in.

If you ever want to invite David for your events, he can be reached through
Email: iamdsimon@gmail.com
LinkedIn: LinkedIn.com/in/dsimonr
Instagram: @iamdsimon

Chapter 4 – On the Other End

Chapter 5

The Path to Impact, Significance, and Success
By Jonah Erbe

  Why do you do what you do? What is the purpose of your career? Do you sometimes feel like you might be going in circles? Do you feel like you are at a dead end? Do you dread going to work every day? I think if we are honest with ourselves, we can all agree we have been there. We have all asked questions about if we are truly where we should be, or if we have fully achieved all that we thought we could be. I firmly believe that the reason we feel this way so frequently is simply because we have no direction. When we go through life wandering aimlessly without direction, how can we possibly achieve our goals and feel any sort of significance? The first step to setting and achieving goals is to develop our own personal 'why' so that we can find our way. My goal is that by the end of this chapter you see that you can achieve goals that you never even thought were possible. I do not want to simply give you another 30-second YouTube clip that promises all your issues will go away if you just perform 5 easy steps. My hope is for you to gain insight to how you can develop yourself to your full potential so you, in turn, can assist others in their development journey. By

Chapter 5 – The Path to Impact, Significance, and Success

developing your own personal 'why' you can find your way, find your purpose, choose your path, and run ever forward into the beautiful unknown without ever looking back.

I remember one of my first real jobs during the summer before my freshman year of high school. I would wake up at 5:30 in the morning, go to football practice, then go straight to work at a water cooler company where my job was to clean and deliver 5-gallon water jugs to companies and houses within a 50-mile radius. It was time-consuming, hard, dirty work, but it paid eight dollars an hour! I was ecstatic that I was making enough money to buy a gallon of sweet tea after work (you read that right: a full gallon of sweet tea). I began that job with a youthful excitement that can only be described as a kid in a candy store. Every day for the first month, I arrived at my job smiling and ready to work. However, about six weeks in, I began to see a drop off in my desire to go to work. When I was headed to work, I would complain and dread the thought of cleaning even one more 5-gallon jug or delivering one jug to the top of a six-story building. Sick and tired of the same old routine day in and day out, I began to have some doubts.

One night after work, I remember going home and asking my dad, "How do you do this every day? How do you get up, go do the same job every day, and stay positive?" My dad was the epitome of consistent faithfulness: He woke up early, studied the Bible, prayed over our family and other loved ones, worked out, went to work, and came home with a smile on his face ready to love on my brother, my mom, and myself no matter how poorly the day had gone. You can understand why I would go to him with my question. Why was I not able to be positive like him when I had only been

Chapter 5 – The Path to Impact, Significance, and Success

doing my job for six weeks? I remember his answer as clearly as if he had said it to me this morning. He said, "What keeps me going is knowing that I am doing it for the Lord. The Lord gave everything for us, so it is my job to give everything I have to Him every day, no matter what I am doing. Remember why you do what you do." This outlook is also seen throughout Scripture in verses like 1 Corinthians 10:31 and Colossians 3:17, 23. From that day on, I have worked to develop my own personal 'why' to guide my life and to filter all of my life's decisions.

It was not always like this, though. Like most people, the wise advice I received earlier in life went straight in one ear and out the other. I did not absorb the true value of my 'why' until college. Throughout high school and the beginning of college, I wrestled with the true meaning of success. On one hand, I knew what the Bible said: money was not the goal and that the love of money was sinful. Outwardly, I put on a strong spiritual front. I would say, "Everything I do is for the glory of God." I even tricked myself into believing that my heart was in the right place. We humans tend to trick ourselves into believing something about ourselves to justify our wrong intentions.

On the other hand, I heard what the world said. I remember watching shows and reading articles about what the richest men in the world were doing and how they spent their money. I remember lying awake in bed thinking about all that I could do with money. I wanted the nice house, the summer home, the country club membership, the new car, the boat, the exotic vacations four times a year, and more! Now, I do want to make sure everyone who reads this knows that money is not evil, nor is possessing nice things. There is

Chapter 5 – The Path to Impact, Significance, and Success

nothing wrong with things. What makes possessions evil is your own personal heart and desire behind them. (1 Timothy 6:10) I believe we should work as hard as we can in everything we do. Sometimes when we work hard, we earn money, and that can buy us nice things. There is nothing wrong with that. However, we should work hard for the glory of God and to impact others, not so that we can make more money to buy ourselves nice things. The possessions are just icing on the cake. Clearly, my intentions were in the wrong place, thus making my desires sinful.

My heart's intentions quickly became known when I began my time at Baylor University. I remember Googling which majors would bring in the most money. All I wanted was the quickest way to make a fortune. Not once did I think about how my studies and education could serve the Lord, but only how I could serve myself. I began trying many different degree paths all in hopes of making the most money possible. I would leave lectures feeling empty, uneasy, and selfish. My thoughts and conversations revolved around furthering myself, not others. I knew this had to change. I needed to discover my 'why.'

Being the incredibly wise college student I was, I declared accounting as my major before ever taking an accounting class. I then figured I should probably take a class in my field of study. Now let me be clear, there is nothing evil about accounting! However, my reasoning for choosing accounting as my major was strictly because it was at the top of the leaderboard of highest average starting salary after graduation. I saw that as my quickest track to making a large sum of money for myself. How hard could it be? All I had to do was make one side of the balance sheet equal out to

Chapter 5 – The Path to Impact, Significance, and Success

the other side. Easy! Well, apparently it is not quite that simple. Let's just say my GPA was less than stellar by the end of that semester. Not only was my GPA struggling, but so was I. My friends who were gifted at accounting were able to breeze through the exams with ease while I was stuck on the first few questions. I would study double the amount of time others did for those exams and still fail. This was incredibly frustrating to me. I was absolutely not gifted in the skill set that goes into being a successful accountant. I quickly erased accounting off my list of how I was going to make money.

That summer, I began watching the show Shark Tank, which is a television show where entrepreneurs present their business ideas to a panel of millionaires to hopefully gain some key investors in their young company. Those who go on the show can make deals worth well over a million dollars. This caught my attention immediately. I thought, *"How hard could it be to start your own company?"* Everyone on the show was making millions of dollars doing it, so I would, too. I took an entrepreneurship class at Baylor quickly after that. I loved the class, but quickly found out that my gifts at the time did not align with starting my own business as a teenager. All I cared about was the end result of pitching to some investors and receiving money. I was not passionate about the process of starting and running the company from scratch. All I saw was the exit strategy with no love for the process leading up to it. Once again, my intentions revolved around personal gain.

I came to a crossroads at this point. What was my purpose? I was terrible at accounting, could not become passionate about entrepreneurship at that point in my life, saw class as a chore, and had no direction. Instead of taking

Chapter 5 – The Path to Impact, Significance, and Success

a step back and allowing myself to be led to the success that God had for me, I thought I needed to pull God down my own path that I was going to pave for myself. I was prideful, I had a chip on my shoulder, and I disguised it by saying it was what God wanted for my life. I was pursuing God's plan for my life in many areas, but not in the area of my professional career. It comes to no surprise that the areas I was letting God lead me in were thriving and the area I refused to let Him take over, I was failing time and time again.

I want to make sure you know what I mean by "failing time and time again." Some people think getting fired, underperforming at work, or missing out on that sale are failure professionally. I disagree. Those are simply moments to learn and improve. Failure is when we cheat ourselves and sell ourselves short on our potential or passions and settle. I was settling, therefore I was failing. Sure, I was achieving great things at my jobs in college. I was selling well, making good money for a college student, and building good relationships in different industries. However, I was doing it all for the wrong reasons, not pursuing my God-given passions, and allowing pride to take over. That is true and total failure. Getting a promotion does not make us successful. Making money does not make us successful. Achieving our full potential to the glory of God to then, in turn, help others reach their full potentials makes us successful. It is absolutely impossible to be successful while thinking about yourself.

I realized I was going nowhere. My 'why' was undeveloped and needed to be set. Knowing that something needed to change, I went to Scripture to discover the truth

Chapter 5 – The Path to Impact, Significance, and Success

about my 'why.' As a Believer, Christ gave us a 'why' in Matthew 28:19-20 when He said, "Go and make disciples of all nations baptizing them in the name of the Father, the Son, and the Holy Spirit, teaching them to observe all that I have commanded you. And behold, I am with you always, to the end of the age." As a Christian, we should view every decision we make in life through this scope with the same focus as that of a sniper. In all we do, we are to make disciples throughout the world.

This Biblical 'why' is incredibly important, and I want to make sure you know that the 'why' God gives us should always trump our own desires. However, I think it is absolutely vital that we, through a Gospel perspective, develop our own, personal 'why' that goes hand in hand with the passage in Matthew. Why do we do what we do? What keeps us going? What is our end goal? What wakes you up in the morning and keeps you awake at night? What passions and desires have been placed on your heart that cannot be quenched? These are questions you must answer. In the words of a wise 102-year-old World War II veteran that I had the pleasure of meeting a few years ago, "Do something you love. Life is too short to pursue something you are not passionate about."

The great philosopher Aristotle once said, "An unexamined life is not worth living." Even someone as wise as Aristotle saw the value in taking time to invest in our own lives. Setting goals and developing your 'why' are vital to finding the path in which we can pursue all that God has called us to do. I do not know about you, but I want to live the life Jesus has called me to live: a life worth living. If you are reading this, then make today the day you begin your life

Chapter 5 – The Path to Impact, Significance, and Success

worth living. Yesterday is in the past and must be forgotten. Tomorrow is not guaranteed and will inevitably be full of inaction and failure if we do not take the necessary steps today. Are you ready to take the necessary steps to develop your 'why' and filtering your life through that lens? If so, then you will begin your life worth living.

After discovering this, I knew I needed to fully develop my own, personal mission statement. My 'why' through which I filter every decision I make, is as follows: "To help others realize and reach their potential physically, mentally, spiritually, professionally, and relationally." Through this, I can filter everything from what I do today, to what I plan to do 30 years down the road. By having a set statement that shapes my life's decisions, I can set up everything I do to inevitably allow me to reach my goal of impacting the most people I possibly can, the best I possibly can. God has given me passions that fire me up. These passions are helping others realize their potential, helping them reach that potential, mourning with people in their failures, and rejoicing with people in their successes. Romans 12:15 says "Rejoice with those who rejoice, weep with those who weep." This is what makes me want to get out of bed in the morning. I am fired up just thinking about it!

By developing my 'why,' I then pursued a new avenue of business in which I knew I had been gifted. I wanted to pursue sales in the sports industry. Where I had struggled in other classes that I thought were best for me, I excelled in all of my classes that tailored to sales. Professionally and educationally, everything was finally clicking. I would go to class excited to learn, reach out to those in the industry simply because I enjoyed learning more

Chapter 5 – The Path to Impact, Significance, and Success

about what they did, and read articles about the latest happenings in the sports industry. I had never done anything like this before. Sure, there were days where I was not excited about it, but that will happen with anything because we are human.

After college, I accepted a job with a professional baseball team. The salary was low, the hours were long, but I had a passion for it. I loved going in to work. I was not making as much money as my friends who had just graduated, but I knew that I was doing something that used my God-given talents to impact people. I also had leadership above me that I was able to learn from every day. Since I enjoyed work, I came home feeling like I had accomplished something and made a difference. My wife noticed how much I loved my job and this brought us even closer together. Everything worked better because I was doing something that aligned with my passions and allowed me to push myself to grow every single day. Even when I had to stay late to visit clients at the ballpark on a Friday night, I could rest assure that I was doing what lined up best with my 'why.' I thought that I would stay with the team forever. However, sometimes God has other plans for our lives.

Out of nowhere, I was offered a job as the Vice President of Marketing with a company called Leadership Management International back in my wife's and my hometown of Waco, Texas. We had just left Waco, moved our lives to Dallas, I was enjoying my job at the baseball team, and we loved where we were at in life. Thankfully, I had already developed my own, personal 'why' through which to examine all of life's decisions, which helped me realize that my goal was to impact the most people I possibly

Chapter 5 – The Path to Impact, Significance, and Success

could. Although I felt like I was making an impact in my current role, I realized that maybe I was not impacting the most people I possibly could. I then began to research the company. I went to LMI's website and stumbled upon their mission statement. When I read it, I had one of those moments where you just have to look up at God and say "nicely done." The mission statement reads, "Developing Leaders and Organizations to their Full Potentials." The way the company is successful is to literally impact the most people they possibly can. If not for my 'why,' I would have stayed where I was and been happy, but not been able to reach my full potential while helping others reach their full potentials.

Now, I am in a company that is currently impacting others in over 80 countries all over the world. I am able to help people develop into their full potentials physically, mentally, spiritually, relationally, and professionally every single day. When we have our 'why' set in place, the possibilities are endless. We no longer exude energy in hundreds of different places, but focus all of our being into one, specific avenue. This allows us to then develop and master our God-given abilities and become successful every day. The beauty of focusing all of our energy down one specific path in which we have been gifted is that we maximize our potential. We do not try to force our weaknesses to be strengths, which can be exhausting. Instead, we pour our blood, sweat, and tears into the specific areas where we have already been gifted. By working towards our 'why,' we can achieve goals that we once never thought imaginable.

Chapter 5 – The Path to Impact, Significance, and Success

When I have had to make decisions, I have been able to filter them through this vision. I was also able to define my own personal success through my 'why.' I decided that my own personal success meant going to bed exhausted every night from the amount of work I put in every day to improve physically, mentally, spiritually, relationally, and professionally. A Biblical reference to my definition of personal success is found in Ecclesiastes 5:12, which states, "Sweet is the sleep of a laborer, whether he eats little or much, but the full stomach of the rich will not let him sleep." Throughout my young career, I have had some job offers that promised worldly benefits, but did they help me achieve my goal, and would they help me reach Biblical success? No. Since I had my 'why' in place, I could quickly turn those offers down knowing that those were not what God had planned for my life. If we do not refocus our lives every day through our 'why,' we will eventually become a slave to whatever sounds correct based on our current emotions. If we make decisions based on temporary feelings, eventually we will be lost with no sense of direction. We will have no idea where we are going, or where we even intend our destination to be. By refocusing our lives every day through a Biblical perspective and our 'why,' we will be able to stay on the path that will most effectively push us forward in our own personal growth. In turn, this will allow us to impact the most people for good.

A person who has been an inspiration to me is a man named Paul J. Meyer. One of his most famous quotes states, "Whatever you vividly imagine, ardently desire, sincerely believe, and enthusiastically act upon, must inevitably come to pass!" Make the decision today to find your 'why' and to

Chapter 5 – The Path to Impact, Significance, and Success

filter all of your decisions through it. This will allow what you most ardently desire to "inevitably come to pass." Dream big in business and in life. Too many people's dreams are incredibly tiny. Do we not know the God we serve? Ephesians 3:20 shows that we serve a God who "is able to do far more abundantly than all that we ask or think, according to the power at work within us." In business and in life, have passion, purpose, and dream massive dreams. Live with a sniper's focus filtered through your 'why' so you can impact the world most effectively.

I have a 'why,' and I hope you do, too. If not, please take some time to develop yours. It may take an hour, a day, a week, or even a month. It will change over time, but make sure to have a specific 'why' set in place so that you can filter life's decisions through it. However, do not stop there.

So many motivational texts and speakers nowadays like to pump us up, make us feel like we are going to change the world, and then leave us there. We discover exactly what our purpose is and we are unbelievably excited for what is to come. We then go back to our job the next day. We let our positive emotions slowly fade away and fall directly back into the dead-end "survival mode" we were in before. We see each day as a task and not as an opportunity to move forward. We go home and let our relationships slip away when we swore we would never let that happen again. Physically we begin to settle for letting ourselves go again. We put down our life-giving Bibles and pick up the most negative news we can find that only make us more depressed. We start to spend more money than we have and go further into debt when we said we were going to attack our debt and get out. What has happened to us? We are worse off than

Chapter 5 – The Path to Impact, Significance, and Success

before we even found our reason for living. How many of us have felt like this? We reach that mountaintop feeling and then quickly stumble down the far side of the mountain into a deep, dark valley of insignificance.

We have been given a life to live to the fullest. God has gifted us with talents and passions to pursue to impact people and bring others to know Him more. We are to help others reach their full potentials as we attempt to reach ours. Surely, we are not to live down in a valley for our entire lives. That is not life to the fullest. You know your 'why,' so why are you settling for anything but achieving your purpose? You have a purpose, you have a reason for living, and you are to make an impact in the world around you. THIS is life to the fullest and a life worth living. Anything less than pursuing your 'why' is an absolute lie that I dare you to not believe. I dare you to believe in the God-given gifts you have been blessed with.

So, you may be asking, "I know my 'why,' I know I have a purpose, but how do I actually make it happen?" This is a great question and one that I cannot answer for you. It is something we all have to answer for ourselves. However, one thing I can assure you is this: Sitting there waiting for the perfect opportunity and situation to come your way to finally get started will NEVER happen. If you live your whole life waiting for the right moment to come your way to achieve your purpose, you will die having left an unbelievable amount of potential behind. I want you to look at the Bible and find one person (besides Jesus, of course) who had it all together before he or she made an impact. Let me save you some time and assure you that you will not find a single

Chapter 5 – The Path to Impact, Significance, and Success

person. To reach our fullest potentials in business and in life, we must start right now.

If Biblical examples are not good enough for you, then how about we look at some of the most successful companies as of late, like Apple, Facebook, Amazon, and Google. Was Steve Jobs sitting there one day when someone walked up to him and let him know that he wanted a phone that could play music, take pictures, access the internet, etc.? No. That is absolutely not how it happened with any of those companies. The founders had to take that first step into the great unknown that is potential success. Did they all experience failures and hardships? Yes. Did they eventually create companies that now change the world because they met a need that they saw that gave them passion? Yes. It is a widely known fact that nine out of every ten new companies that are founded fail within the first three years. Why then do so many people continue to become entrepreneurs? I think the answer is something like this: People are fed up with wandering aimlessly through life. We all have a desire to make a difference and to change the world. We all need to come to a point where we are fed up with simply strolling through life without making an impact. We must use our 'why' to develop our way. Once we do this, the possibilities are endless.

John C. Maxwell said it best in his book, "The Power of Significance: How Purpose Changes Your Life," when he said, "If you want to make a difference and live a life of significance, you find your why. You need to tap into your purpose. I'm certain everybody has one. Your why is the life's blood of your ability to achieve significance. If you know your why and focus on going there with fierce

Chapter 5 – The Path to Impact, Significance, and Success

determination, you can make sense of everything on your journey because you see it through the lens of why. Once you find your why, you will be able to find your way. How do those things differ? Why is your purpose. Way is your path."

From my studies, I have found that the most effective path to finding your way is to lay out your goals in front of you. Write out your one year, two-year, five-year, ten-year, and twenty-year goals. Set long-term goals that are specific, measurable, achievable, realistic, and timely. Send them off to a few people that know you well and have them read over them and send back their insights. Ask those people to keep you accountable and walk through life with you. Then, find a mentor that will guide you along in life and business. Once you have done this, begin to take it day-by-day. Set goals for yourself every day and week. This will allow you to daily achieve progress towards your long-term goals. Since you have a 'why,' you can filter every single goal, whether short-term or long-term. This will allow you to steadily hit goals and stay in tune with your vision and values. Before you know it, you will have made more progress than you can possibly imagine and will have found a way to your 'why.'

Now that you have found your 'why,' and your way, I challenge you to make progress towards your way every single day. Do not wait until tomorrow or until the perfect moment presents itself. Take that first step in faith and trust that you have the God-given potential to make a difference and achieve success. Too many people today wait idly, expecting success to come to them instead of going on the offensive and making it happen. No matter what has

Chapter 5 – The Path to Impact, Significance, and Success

happened in the past, what is happening right now, or what may come in the future, believe that you can, and will, achieve your full potential. Focus on improving every day. Set daily goals for yourself to hit your long-term goals. Success will follow, and most importantly, you will make an impact.

"What lies behind us and what lies before us are tiny matters compared to what lies within us."

- Ralph Waldo Emerson

Chapter 5 – The Path to Impact, Significance, and Success

About the Author – Jonah Erbe

Jonah Erbe is the Vice President of Marketing for Leadership Management International, a global leadership and business development company located in Waco, Texas. Their mission is to develop leaders and organizations to maximize their full potential. Jonah views everything he does through his personal mission statement, "To help others realize and reach their potential physically, mentally, spiritually, professionally, and relationally." Jonah resides in Waco, Texas with his loving wife, and high school sweetheart, Brooke. Together, they have been married for one year. There are no children in the picture yet, but their golden retriever, Duke, keeps them busy. Jonah graduated from Baylor University with a BBA in Sports Sponsorship and Sales. While in college, Jonah was a youth pastor at a church in Waco where he developed a love for helping others realize their potential through who Jesus has called us to be, as well as a love for business. After graduating he decided to combine his love for serving others and business to achieve his goal of bringing the Gospel to the world of business.

You can reach Jonah at

LinkedIn: www.linkedin.com/in/jonaherbe/
Instagram: @jonaherbe
Email: jerbe@lmi-inc.com

Chapter 5 – The Path to Impact, Significance, and Success

Chapter 6

Love Is the Answer
By Maggie Castor

My Father was my hero. He passed away in December of 2017 at the age of 90. He worked until he was 88. My Dad was a man of high character. He was 100% Italian, and Dad and my Mother raised our family in an Italian neighborhood just outside the city of Philadelphia. We lived right next door to my Grandparents and down the street from a bunch of our relatives.

Dad was an honest, hard-working guy who had an easygoing personality. He had a quiet type of wisdom, mainly passed along in how he lived his life and occasionally passed along in the form of what I would call "an Italian parable" in bits of wisdom like, "An empty bag can't stand up." Or like the story Dad would tell with a smile and in his good-natured way, "A son and his father were going up to the mountain one day. The son says to his father, 'Pop, you don't work—but you eat, you drink. What am I going to do with you?' The father says to the son, 'One day you will get old, too.' So then they both walked back down the mountain together." In his late seventies, Dad would start kidding with us, saying things like, "I signed up for a 100, and if I don't make it, I'm suing." And then he would start to laugh. Or he might say, "What I'm living now, I'm stealing," and we would all laugh.

Chapter 6 – Love Is the Answer

That comment was even funnier because Dad was an honest person.

Dad was a Landscape Gardener, a trade his Father, my Pop-Pop, taught him, and he worked from the age of 13. Pop-Pop immigrated to the U.S. in 1917 at the age of 17. Amazingly, my Pop-Pop came here to the United States alone, not knowing the language, and with very little money. He had heard that "the streets were paved in gold." There was little work in Italy at the time, and people were walking around hungry. My Pop-Pop had a deep faith in God, and he was determined. He immigrated to the United States looking for an opportunity for a much better life. After he immigrated, he was drafted in the US Army, worked as a cook, then briefly as a coal miner. Later, he started working as a Landscape Gardener. Within a span of ten years he served in the military, got married, bought a home, learned how to speak English and had four children. The older that I get, the more I admire the tenacity and persistence of my Grandfather. Seven of his twelve brothers and sisters eventually immigrated here, and several of them lived near us. Needless to say, our family had a lot of ties to Italy. Dad was stationed there on peacekeeping duty for a year. An Italian guy's dream come true. He loved Italy and almost stayed there after WW2. After his duty ended in Northern Italy, Dad wanted to stay and live, but my Pop-pop insisted that he come home. My Pop-Pop needed Dad to work with him in the family's Landscaping business, so Dad went back home to Pennsylvania.

An old-school Italian gardener is an artist. They seek, create, and enjoy the beauty in nature and share it with others. My Grandfather and my Dad were both good-

Chapter 6 – Love Is the Answer

natured and shared a tremendous work ethic. They worked 6 days-a-week, always taking Sundays off. An 86-year-old neighbor nearby my parents home still maintains her large garden herself; she's a tiny Italian woman, but a powerhouse, and has a work ethic a lot like my Father and Grandfather had. My Dad's work spoke volumes about who he was. Dad worked hard, but took time to enjoy the nature around him while he worked. Every day at work, Dad took a short break to enjoy his lunch and a beer. Mom always packed Dad and my Pop Pops lunch, which included one beer for lunch and one beer at the end of the workday. Occasionally, Dad would go to the Village Deli for a steak sandwich or Italian hoagie, but that was not the norm. Dad loved a good meal. His eyes would twinkle if you made him lasagna. If you made him a hamburger, he would say in his charming Italian way, "That was the best burger I ever ate." The funny thing is, he really meant that. When it was Thanksgiving, Dad always found his way into the kitchen for a tiny sample of the meal to come. In a slightly mischievous way, Dad would help himself to an early sampling of Mom's homemade stuffing. He would get to his prize and then retreat from the kitchen, laughing in a good-natured way as we chased him away. My Mom was a great cook. She made "gravy" every Sunday, like clockwork. As a family, we mainly ate at home with the vegetables from our Garden. I think that there is nothing better than having a vegetable and flower garden in your backyard. The vegetables are really fresh and very accessible. My Mom and my Grandmother would pick vegetables from our garden. We had plenty to share with whoever came along to visit. Looking back, being raised in our Italian neighborhood with my sisters, Mary and Terrie, was really an awesome place to grow up. As I get older, I have an even

Chapter 6 – Love Is the Answer

greater respect and honor for my Grandfather and my Father and how really wonderful they were.

"I am quite confident that the one who began a good work in you will go on completing it until the Day of Jesus Christ comes." Philippians 1:6

Both my parents were both positive and encouraging. My Dad would often compliment me on a job well done, saying for example, "Look what Margie did." My Parents instilled a lot of confidence in me, and I knew how much they loved me. If I was dressed up more than usual, Dad would say, "Margie, (my nickname growing up), you look like a million dollars." Dad had an Italian charm about him, but you wouldn't consider him to be charming. His roots ran deeper than that. Dad was great to be around. He would be walking around the house singing songs like "Daddy's Little Girl" or he would sing romantic songs to my Mom like "Lady of Spain." We used to tell people that our Dad sounded like Frank Sinatra. We were all proud of him. Dad actually made a handful of records when he was in his twenties. Humble as he was, he only sang to our family. I loved when Dad would sing. I can still picture Dad coming down the stairs in our house, singing to us. I always knew how much my Father loved me, and loving gestures like this cemented all of the positive and encouraging words that my Dad spoke to me.

I learned so much from my Dad, and I loved spending time with him. Dad was the type of Dad that you could sit on the front porch with, not say many words, but he would seemingly say everything. Dad loved life's simple pleasures, like a good meal, going to Mass, and taking a nice Sunday drive with our family. Dad was the best at living, as the

Chapter 6 – Love Is the Answer

Italians say, "La dolce vita" or "The good life." Amazingly enough, Dad never had a credit card and he paid cash for everything. Dad was authentic and aspired to just be himself. He was a great Patriarch to our family. Dad and Mom have 23 Grandchildren, and to date, 16 Great-grandchildren, and that number is growing. Dad knew everyone's birthday and age. If anyone forgot someone's birthday, they would ask Dad. Even until the age of 89, Dad knew everyone in our extended family's age and birthday. Dad took the time to ask everyone how you were doing if you came to visit. Then, he would ask about your family, name each of them, and ask how they were doing. Then he would say, "Tell them I was asking for them." If you spent time around Dad, you knew how much he cared for you.

> ***"Joy is a net of love by which you can catch souls." Mother Teresa***

My Dad and my Mother loved each other a lot. Dad used to say things to us like, "Your Mom is a nice girl" or "The old gray mare isn't what she used to be," and then laugh in a beautifully affectionate way, which told you really how much Dad really loved Mom. Dad also would say things in an authoritative way like, "Take care of Mom." He probably said that 100 times to all of us, mainly over the past few years. He didn't like the fact that Mom was 8 years younger than him. Dad loved Mom and didn't want to leave her behind. My Mom used to call Dad "Charles Atlas." Dad was strong, due to the nature of his work. Healthy almost his entire life, he didn't drink in excess and he never smoked. About a year before Dad died, he caught a cold. The cold quickly turned to pneumonia and Dad ended up in the hospital, a place foreign to Dad most of his life. Dad's

Chapter 6 – Love Is the Answer

mantra in life had always been "Stay away from the doctor." After Dad was released from the hospital, his cardiologist said that Dad's heart had been adversely affected from his illness. We spent the last year of Dad's life trying to keep him as healthy as possible. Dad ended up going to the hospital several times over the course of the year. It was a difficult year at times for Dad, and for all of us. On one of Dad's hospital visits, my Mom ended up being hospitalized as well. She had gone to visit Dad, but slipped and fell. Mom was admitted for about a week, but for the first 5 days, my Mom and Dad were unable to visit each other. Dad and Mom were never apart from each other for very long. Five days was an eternity for them. Some of the hospital workers happened to witness their reunion. Mom and Dad were like teenagers in love, or as a nurse later told me, like a scene from *The Notebook*. After Mom and Dad's reunion, they were crying - even the nurses were crying. You could see how much they loved each other. Mom and Dad usually made an impression when they went places, especially as they got older. One caregiver actually said to me, "Your Mom and Dad are one in a million." When Mom and Dad were being discharged from their dual hospital visit, you could tell how fond some of the staff members had become of them. It was a wonderful sight: Mom and Dad with balloons and flowers in tow, a nurse saying to some other nurses, "Adele is leaving!" Mom and Dad were like celebrities there. They touched a lot of people's hearts, because they loved each other and the people around them. Dad and Mom were very close to God, and they said short little prayers often. One of Mom's favorite short prayers in recent years is "Show us the Way." I always say that my Mom is all about love. Mom has a great reverence for the Blessed Trinity - The Father, and the Son, Jesus Christ, and the Holy Spirit. Whether they

Chapter 6 – Love Is the Answer

were in a hospital, or at home, Dad and Mom's faith in God showed up in their actions.

"With God, all things are possible." Matthew 19:26

My parent's strong faith in God had an enormous impact on my life. This gift of faith, combined with the tenacity and persistence of both my Grandfather and Father, has been a saving grace throughout my life. In 1999, I went back to school at The University of Arizona to finish my bachelor's degree. I was a single mom at the time, and I was determined to adequately support my family. I had been a "stay-at-home" mom for 16 years doing what I have always loved the most, to take care of my children. My daughter, Heather, and my sons, Joe and Reills, are the most significant blessings in my life. Then, as a single parent, I had to make sure that I could provide for everything that my children and I needed. It was a tough year, but I was determined. My parents were 100% supportive. I'll never forget the card that they gave me after I graduated. It said on the front cover, "And the dreamer began to climb." Though some people kind of scoffed at my intention to find a "dream job," I didn't want to settle for anything else but what I knew in my heart was possible. One of the bright spots for me was joining the University of Arizona Triathlon Club. I loved spending time training with other Tricats; they were a great group of positive, high-achievers. They became one of the sources of support for us, an extended family of sorts. I graduated later that year in December. Prior to graduation, one of my friends introduced me to my future business partner. He was looking for a new partner to help him grow the Sports Nutrition Company that he had started with his brothers. I was elated. I knew this was the dream job I was looking for. I was

Chapter 6 – Love Is the Answer

grateful to God for answering my prayers. I could now provide for my family. My faith was the saving grace on what had been a terribly difficult year.

> ***"Yes, I know what plans I have in mind for you, Yahweh declares, plans for peace, not for disaster, to give you a future and a hope." Jeremiah 29:11***

My business partner and I were both Christians and often shared faith-based stories. We soon became good friends. Our strong faith became the foundation on which we built our new business. My business partner and I were fortunate to hire a talented group of athletes. We would all train together and we had a lot of fun. My business partner had a lot of great stories, so we laughed a lot despite the fact that we were a startup and tight for cash at times. From early morning bikes rides to Sat morning runs in the desert, we would brainstorm about the business. We also traveled to promote our sports nutrition products. As a working single parent, it was really wonderful that my kids and their friends were able to help at some of the expos. My kids were all athletes and involved in sports at the time. It was great for them to be in this type of environment.

Our sports nutrition team accomplished a lot over the course of 8 years. God was always there when we needed Him. My faith grew a lot during this time, and in 2005, It was a tremendous blessing to meet my husband Kelly, who was a friend of my business partner. Three years later, our company sold our brand to one of our customers. We had planned on keeping and growing the manufacturing end of the business, but due to the financial downturn later that year, we lost contracts that we needed for our new business

Chapter 6 – Love Is the Answer

venture. Working in the field of Sports Nutrition had been an incredible experience, but it was now time to move on. This chapter was closing, but another was opening. In the fall of 2008, Kelly and I got married and soon started working on a Christian community garden project together. Kelly and I, along with a good friend, started a nonprofit. One of the programs was a "farm to food bank" model that enabled the underserved in our community to eat more fresh produce, directly supplied from church gardens. It was wonderfully fulfilling work, and very apropos. My Grandfather and Father's gardening heritage was springing up in an awesome and unforeseen way.

"We know that in everything God works for good with those who love him, who are called according to his purpose." Romans 8:28

My Dad and my husband Kelly became close friends soon after they met in 2005. They loved to watch John Wayne movies together and talk about antique cars. They shared a lot of laughs and you could tell that they really enjoyed each other's company. My husband Kelly is from Indiana, and often tells people where he is from by saying, "I come from a town 12 miles from a town of 1200." I had never visited Southern Indiana before we got married. I had also never seen so many cornfields, which was where the church we got married was located. The church had special significance for Kelly's family. The church was next to his Grandfathers farm, where Kelly and his brother Kevin spent a lot of time growing up. My father and mother in law, Don and Carol, had been married at Bear Creek Church 54 years earlier. We decided to get married there, though we considered getting married in the Church where I was raised. Since we were

Chapter 6 – Love Is the Answer

already living near my hometown, Kelly and I thought it would be nice to get married in the town where Kelly was raised. It turned out to be the perfect place for our wedding, surrounded by both of our families - and a lot of corn. Kelly's Uncle Dale married us, an all-around great guy. He's helped a lot of people in his community, and often shares with others how having a personal relationship with Jesus changed his life. A month after our wedding, Kelly and I went to Italy for our honeymoon. I was pretty excited about going, since Italy is where my Pop-Pop was from, and my Dad loved it there. We had a great time in Italy, and more significantly, Italy is where our Gospel Box Ministry would eventually begin.

"Finally, brethren, whatever is true, whatever is honorable, whatever is right, whatever is pure, whatever is lovely, whatever is of good repute, if there is any excellence and if anything worthy of praise, dwell on these things." Philippians 4:8.

Kelly and I got involved with a marriage enrichment group that we found out about at our Church in the summer of 2013. I remembered that a married couple that I really admired when I was a teenager taught marriage classes. My sister and I used to babysit for this couple, and they stood out to me from other couples. Kelly and I decided to sign up for a marriage enrichment weekend that we saw in our church bulletin. We ended the weekend by restating our marriage vows and a Priest blessed our marriage. We told our family and friends about our marriage immersion experience and encouraged them to go on a weekend. We kind of became poster children for marriage enrichment. We grew closer from the experience because it helped us understand

Chapter 6 – Love Is the Answer

each other better. Our time invested in our relationship was taking us to a new level. It was keeping our focus on having a relationship with God first, then each other, then ourselves. We stayed in touch with a group of the couples that we met during the weekend, and later that year joined one of the local marriage enrichment groups, which gathered on a monthly basis. Looking back, it was what God was calling us to do to help prepare us for our Gospel Box Ministry, to have a closer unity.

"The Gospel Box Project"

In September of 2013, Kelly and I were excited that we were able to return to Italy to celebrate our 5th Wedding Anniversary. Pope Francis had been newly elected that March, and he was becoming a popular Pope. I prayed to the Holy Spirit before we planned our trip. We arrived in Rome on the day of our Anniversary, September 6th. We were surprised to find out that Pope Francis would be holding a special prayer service for peace in the Middle East, the next day. A local Priest had told us about it on Friday, the day that we arrived. It was set to be a 4-hour prayer service, something that he said was unprecedented in the years that this Priest had lived in Rome. God has great timing. The prayer service was on Saturday, September 7th, and we were leaving on Sunday to travel to a different part of Italy. We were planning to be back in Rome the day before we left Italy to attend the Wednesday audience where the Pope holds Mass. St Peter's Square is a magnificent place. We felt grateful to be there for our anniversary. The prayer service was beautiful and we felt fortunate to be able to be there to pray for peace with the Pope and all the visitors from all over the world. The next day we made our way via

Chapter 6 – Love Is the Answer

train up to Assisi. Then, we took a car to the village of Assisi. After we checked into our hotel, we walked around the town a bit, then headed over to the Basilica of St Francis of Assisi, which actually had just closed for the day. The caregiver mentioned to us that the Chapel below the Church was open still. We felt compelled to go there. Once there, we found out that this Chapel holds the remains of St Francis of Assisi in a type of Urn on the altar. There was a small group of monks and a handful of other people present for Vespers, which are evening prayers that are sung. Visiting the Basilica was a deeply spiritual experience. When we were in Siena, we went to a church where there are some of the remains of Saint Catherine of Siena. St. Catherine is one of the two Patron Saints of Italy. She was born in Siena and died in Rome in the year 1380. She was known to have spent a lot of time at San Domenico when she lived in Siena. The trip was turning into a sort of a Pilgrimage. After leaving San Domenico, Kelly was convinced that God wanted him to work more with his hands.

Back in Rome on Wednesday, Kelly and I were headed to the weekday Mass that Pope Francis traditionally holds when he is in Rome, except during some of the summer months. We arrived three hours early to St Peter's Square where the Mass was going to be held. It's a very friendly crowd, consisting of people from many different countries on any given Wednesday. St Peter's Square evokes a sense of awe. It's steeped in history, and it was a very peaceful place, despite the large crowds and warm temperature. Everyone seemed pretty elated at the thought of seeing the recently elected Pope. We got even more excited when we found out that Pope Francis would be passing by close to where we were located. I think Kelly and

Chapter 6 – Love Is the Answer

I were both thinking a similar thought—how did we end up here?? We smiled big. Thank you, Jesus! Then, with a lot of fanfare, a bunch of white doves, and an ecstatic crowd, Pope Francis soon came down our little makeshift alley that had been carved out with a line of hobbyhorse type barricades. We were counting our blessings—and crying. It was pretty awesome to be so close to the Pope and it was completely unexpected. After Pope Francis passed by us, one of the guards mentioned that Pope Francis wouldn't pass this way again, that he never comes back through the same route. But a few minutes later, Pope Francis came towards us again-- this time coming over to shake the hand of the little boy who was right next to me. Kelly captured this all on video and got a great picture of Pope Francis. We left Rome the next day ecstatic, overwhelmed, and very grateful.

> *"Christian love is concrete. To love with deeds, not words. Words are taken away by the wind--here today, tomorrow not." Pope Francis, January 2014*

About a month after our anniversary trip, it was October, and we were visiting Kelly's parents. Kelly happened to notice something familiar on one of my Mother-in-law's bookshelves. A small plastic replica of a loaf of bread filled with colorful cards that have Bible verses printed on them. Kelly hadn't seen it in a while. On our way back home, this little box stuck in Kelly's mind, and we started talking about it. Kelly wondered, what if we made our own version of a scripture box? We started brainstorming about it together on our trip back home, thinking that maybe we needed to make a lot of these little boxes.

Over the course of the following year, Kelly and I worked

Chapter 6 – Love Is the Answer

together on our Gospel Box Project. It took about a year to design and manufacture our Gospel Boxes. We had weekly meetings about the progress that we were making on our mutually assigned tasks. We were both working on the design of the Gospel Box. Then we soon found a manufacturer to cut and carve the small wooden boxes. Kelly did the finishing work on them. I prayerfully picked the Bible verses over the course of several months. In October of 2014, we printed 325,000 Gospel Box small brown verse cards that were double-sided, and then we assembled our Gospel Boxes. Our Gospel Boxes were ready just in time for Christmas. Some of them we gave to our family and friends as gifts. Some people bought them as gifts for other people. Some of the Gospel Boxes we've used for Church youth groups to help them promote Bible reading and to also raise donations for their mission trips. Most of the 1800 Gospel Boxes, or about 235,000 verse cards distributed to date, have been donated to various people and different programs. Kelly and I hope to continue to print and distribute many more Gospel verse cards because the wisdom of the Bible is God's loving answer to inspire hope for all mankind.

One of my favorite uses of the Gospel Box was donating verse cards to an outreach program in North Carolina. Sr. Mary Isaac, who is well respected in the community, had been helping the poor in Wilmington, NC for over 30 years. Sister Mary Isaac's Outreach provides food, clothing, and household items for people in need. Occasionally, they provide payment of overdue rent and utility bills. Sister used the Gospel Box verse cards to minister to her clients. I worked weekly with Sister for a couple of years, and it was

Chapter 6 – Love Is the Answer

one of my most favorite experiences. I met a lot of very grateful people, filled with a deep faith in God. In 2011, Sister had received an award from Pope Benedict for her outstanding help to the poor. Sister retired a couple of years ago from the ministry, which now bears her name. She started the ministry when someone came to her door in need of help.

"My dear children, let us not love in word, neither with the tongue, but in deed and in truth." I John 3:18

I heard a well-known pastor once comment that he thought that God might ask us two questions after we die: "Did you love?" and "Did you tell others about me?"

Jesus tells us directly about the overall importance of loving actions and deeds in our life in the Gospel of Matthew: *"And one of them, a doctor of the Law, putting him to the test, asked him, "Master, which is the great commandment in the Law?" Jesus said to him, "'Thou shalt love the Lord thy God with thy whole heart, and with thy whole soul, and with thy whole mind.' This is the greatest and the first commandment. And the second is like it, 'Thou shalt love thy neighbor as thyself.' On these two commandments depend the whole Law and the Prophets."* Matthew 22:35-40

I think that we all make decisions from moment to moment on how we are going to treat the people around us. My Parents set a tremendous example on how to love those around us. I have seen the difference it makes when I choose to love the people that God puts in front of me. Jesus modeled a radically inclusive love, and Jesus invites us to follow His example. *"Jesus said, I am the WAY; I am truth and life. No one can come to the Father except through me."* John 14:6

Chapter 6 – Love Is the Answer

We are free to choose to answer God with a "yes" or "no" on whether we choose to love the people that God puts right in our path. Let's choose to say yes.

Chapter 6 – Love Is the Answer

About the Author – Maggie Castor

Maggie is the Co-foundress of Mission Water, and has spent the last nine years focusing on faith-based initiatives to improve the quality of life for the poor, including poverty relief, clean water initiatives, and evangelization. In 2009, Maggie launched a Catholic Community Garden project that was later studied by Cardinal Peter Turkson, President of the Pontifical Council for Justice and Peace, under the Papacy of Pope Francis. Prior to her work in the non-profit sector, Maggie led at the C-level in the Functional Foods Industry for eight years as a dynamic, creative, and passionate team motivator.

Maggie and her husband Kelly both are excited about their latest project-Co-launching an Atlanta-based Christian Music studio with their family. They are also facilitating "The Marriage Course," www.themarriagecourse.org, a series of seven sessions, designed for couples that want to invest in their relationship and build a stronger marriage. The course is based on Christian principles but designed for all couples with or without a church background.

Maggie has a BA in Psychology/Nutrition from the University of Arizona, where she was a member of the triathlon team.

Chapter 6 – Love Is the Answer

Maggie and her husband Kelly are very blessed to have two awesome sons, Joe and Reills and a daughter, Heather, who is married to her college sweetheart, Jeff. Maggie and Kelly are members of Passion City Church and serve on their Worship Music Production team.

Reach out and connect with Maggie through social media via LinkedIn: Linkedin.com/in/philanthropymissionwater/ Instagram: @maggiemcastor or through the website www.missionwater1.org

Chapter 7

Strategic Storm
By Addison Baker

-Nothing is ever by coincidence-

A strategic storm is said to only happen every blue moon (as older people used to tell me when I was a little boy), but it sets the trajectory of something greater to come... I'm not sure why... but here goes...

UNCOMMON: It Just So Happened

It is a miracle within itself that I am alive and functioning. I was born in the early 70's into a country area to parents who believed in the anointing oil and the power of healing.

When I was age four, I stumbled into a cabinet at home which contained a box of lye used in the old days for making soap and cleaning products. Being the busy-body that I was, I ingested some of it. The lye ate my vocal cords, among other things! I lost my sight and use of motor skills. The lye had eaten my facial skin.

The mothers of the church came and prayed, pouring anointing oil on me. And in three days God healed me by actually growing and replacing my vocals cords and restoring the peeling skin without scarring. I remember not being able to speak or see, but miraculously God showed His hand and plan for my life.

Not only that, I was born with asthma, but God healed me from severe asthmatic attacks at the age of 12. So, I am really saying, I didn't have the breath nor the vocals, but God gave them to me for His glory.

As a result of His goodness and kindness, I promised Him that with every breath I take and with my voice lifted in thanksgiving, I will praise Him!

I tell this testimony because it set the trajectory of my life. I grew up believing the impossible. It may sound far-fetched to some, or even downright unbelievable to others. However, when you have an encounter, not just an experience with God, you will never be the same. You can't unknow what you know, it is just something that marks your life monumentally. Thus, I write to you, **the disbeliever, the healed, and the scarred…**

RESERVED WITH PURPOSE: The Moses Story

I'm sure the beginning part sounds rosy and glorious, but let's back up the story a moment to place it into some context.

My mother became a missionary and had fallen in love with my dad who, at the time, had not been called into the ministry. He was a hard worker but very strong-willed or cantankerous. It was prophesied that my mother would have another child after the death or her eldest son (he was not of this marriage, and he had been shot and killed weeks before his wedding by a jealous ex). Compounded with the death of

Chapter 7 – Strategic Storm

a son, depression, and health issues, the announcement of my birth caused a breakdown for my mother. She bore me at age 42 (which mom called 'out of due season') into a "unique family." My dad believed that I was not his child. This created a lot of family tension. He often threatened to harm me if she brought that "bastard" home.

So, the strategic plan of God had begun to unfold. As I got older, I believe God spoke to me and said, "I hid you like Moses," during a meditation moment. I had forgotten this all these years until a few years ago, when speaking with my sister. Some things you wipe out of your mind or put in the furthest, deepest crevice until you are able to deal with it in time.

Because of my dad's rage, I was taken after birth to be raised by some of my mother's friends. I remember growing up in a huge three-story home on a hill with French velvet curtains and mahogany woodwork throughout. This French lady, who had become like a mom to me, named me Addison, although I had siblings with Bible names; a brother named John and a sister named Elizabeth. I never knew why I didn't get a Bible name, like James, until I was older. She had been a singer overseas and traveled with her music group before marrying and moving to the states. This was a set-up for my calling which came later in music ministry. She carried a mantle which would become mine – I would tour and sing with a music group as I grew older.

There is a timing of God that He uses to piece your story together. No matter how terrible things are, YOU will live to declare the glory of God. You are God's child and you belong. There is a place for you!

Chapter 7 – Strategic Storm

So, to **those who have ever felt like you don't belong, homeless, orphan, destitute or unwanted,** this is for you…

DOES GOD EVEN LIKE ME? Well, He loved ME

Then the day finally came when I was to be introduced to my real family once again at the age of four. Life would never be the same!

I found that my mother was a clairvoyant woman with a gift of knowledge who had married a man called to ministry but not yet surrendered to God. They were an odd couple, if I say so myself. After the lye incident, my mom carried me with her everywhere she went. During that time, God began to deal with me in my faith and the supernatural (once you come back from the jaws of death, life seems a little weird and more than the natural). However, I didn't know that there was something more extraordinary about to happen.

I remember: I was outside playing in the dirt, as boys do, when a strange visitor came up to meet me. At the time, I thought it was normal, but he, or it, looked very different than any other person that I had ever seen or known. I went flying into the kitchen where my dad was sitting, and I told him that someone was outside to see him. My dad got up and strolled outside to meet the person. I am not quite sure what happened or what was said, I just remember my dad running back into the house and sitting as if he had seen a ghost. I believed then and now know it was an angel of God. I have not encountered another experience as such! Not long after,

Chapter 7 – Strategic Storm

my dad began preaching and became a pastor by the time I turned age seven.

As time progressed, I joined the church at age seven and professed my belief in Christ. I was singing in the junior choir and was given my first lead in a song, "Jesus is My Keeper." No one had really ever heard me sing until I stepped up to the microphone, which became a defining moment. In the interim, I had become a member of my family's home church before dad began pastoring. Eventually, I began attending my dad's church every other Sunday. This was the start of singing and evangelizing with my family as a PK (pastor's kid).

One day, a woman walked into the foyer of my home church and said (prophetically), "You are going to preach." I told her (as uncommon as it was for children during that time to talk back to adults, especially at age seven), "I am going to forever sing!" and walked away hoping that I wouldn't get a knot yanked in my neck collar by my mom. I only knew or understood at the time that I did not and was not going to be like some of the preachers that I knew or had seen (I had become scarred at age seven and didn't know why). However, God knows the plans for your life, even when we err and fall short. (Jeremiah 29:11) His plans are good and not evil, and they are to fulfill the work in you that He began before and while you were in your mother's womb. (Philippians 1:6)

By age 17, I had been called into the ministry. I have noticed through time that God does have a sense of humor. Can not the one who created the smile, laugh? I met the lady from the foyer who had spoken over my life years later in a clothing store. She knew me as she walked over to me and said, "You're preaching now, aren't you?" All I could say was, "Yes, ma'am." That was the last I saw of her. She died three months later, however, she lived to see God fulfill His word in my life.

Coming up on my senior year of high school, I had planned to hide any fact of being called into the ministry. Of course, what would my friends say? NOT COOL. I would rather just be the playboy and wander aimlessly into my own ways. NOT SO. Later in my senior year, I was recommended by my school administration to be a highlight in the state newspaper on rising High School graduates. I was awarded various scholarships, so I had planned to speak on my achievements. But *they had heard* that I had been recently assigned as youth pastor at my family church and wanted to do a full spread on the front page of their High School Profiles. NOOOOOOOOOOOOOOOOOOOO, not that! "*Now everyone will know,*" I thought.

I toughed it out with a smile and they did a full layout on the front AND part of the back of the newspaper. My life was over as I knew it. I could feel God smiling, as if to say, "You thought you could hide from me, but I am pursuing you!"

I speak to the **unqualified yet qualified by God, to the introverted at heart, or the forgotten and reluctant....** All things are working for His glory!

Meanwhile, things were like Saul and David in my home. My father and I were at odds, but we learned to have an estranged mutual rapport when dealing in ministry, just not with each other. He would often do unthinkable things just to set us at odds. He became very dark, even cold and distant. "But why… what did I ever do to you?" I would ask

Chapter 7 – Strategic Storm

myself. Sometimes people can only give to you what they have been given. In other words, HURT PEOPLE, HURT PEOPLE.

Things became so bad that I remember standing and looking down on my dad while he was sleeping. Angry and confused, yet I heard God once more, "Touch not mine anointed and do my prophet no harm," Really, God? Really… But You see how I'm being mistreated like the black sheep of the family (As I grew older, I later discovered that my dad was raised by his step-father. The man who was my dad's biological father – my grandfather – had been a prominent man and pastor in the community. We even fellowshipped at his church when I was a child. My dad even preached a few times at his father's church, but no one ever stated that this man was my grandfather. We lived down the street from him all those years. When he passed, dad was included in *his* will. I understood a little piece more. My grandfather was named "James.") But let me continue the story…

I decided then and there I would graduate with honors and scholarships to move out on my own by age 21. That graduation year, I received five scholarships and was placed on the honor roll, only to find out that my father had disapproved of my college and set forth plans to hinder its processing. This made me more independent and I moved in with my sister at age 21. Many things happened between life. I can't explain why we, as people, do the things we do. As I grew older, I was confronted with an unknown family estate which was a harmful cause to the hiding of illegitimate children. Due to the circumstances and safety at this time, it protected the innocence of family heirs. Oh, the sins of the

Chapter 7 – Strategic Storm

fathers which carry to their children and leave them wayward or on edge. For lack of depth, I became wayward and continued the broken cycle as my father and his before. I will keep it simple… my children are not my children.

This is **to any father or parent who wished to raise their child and could not for some reason. To those unable to see their child or children grow up. To those imprisoned and can't see their children or to those who watched as your child called another "Dad" or "Mom"** … this is for you…

It was good that I was afflicted. At about age 25, God spoke to my heart saying, "Get your house in order, for I will come quickly." This was not a comforting statement at this moment in my life. God was calling me back to holiness. However, this was a rebuke and I knew it! I had fallen prey to sin and did not want God to take me in my waywardness. I had been reading about Hezekiah in the book of Isaiah and I understood that His words to me were a strong reference to repent. Three days before my twenty-fifth birthday, my apartment was broken into. I had had a dream the night before but did not understand the full reference. But it was enough to make me pray and repent on my face before God. The day of the break-in, my boss asked me to stay later to help finish some work. This particular time, I was leaving work at 6:30 p.m. (I usually arrived home by 6:30 p.m.). God protected me. I always kept an alarm clock by my bed. When the thieves were ravishing the room, they knocked the table over, unplugging the clock. The time the alarm clock stopped at read 6:30 p.m. If I had come home earlier from work, I would have walked in on the thieves, which probably would have resulted in fatality. But this was not to be my end.

Chapter 7 – Strategic Storm

I had started fasting and praying the following week. About two weeks later, after the break-in, I would meet one of the assailants who broke into my home. He proclaimed to have been paid and now had been threatened if he snitched. However, he said that he felt compelled to come to my home and ask for forgiveness. He was a member of a gang and said as part of their initiation they had planned to take a life that night of the break-in. READ CLOSELY: I WAS TALKING TO THE MAN THAT WAS ASSIGNED TO TAKE MY LIFE, BUT HE FELT COMPELLED TO ASK ME FOR FORGIVENESS. God is simply amazing! Before we completed our conversation, he confessed many things. I anointed and prayed for this man like never before! He accepted Christ in the middle of my living room. He came to take life but found LIFE!

To the **gang member or the addicted (whatever the sin)...** He can get or bring you out! We all have sinned and missed the mark of righteousness. (Romans 3:23) However, there is redemption from our mess! "If My people who are called by My name will humble themselves, and pray and seek My face, and turn from their wicked ways, then I will hear from heaven, and will forgive their sin, and heal their land." (2 Chronicles 7:14) Prayer still works. God still answers prayer!

Sometimes life can leave you in shambles and shame until it makes you feel as if you stood in the line labeled "PROBLEMS HERE" and you were picked to suffer while everyone else went on their merry little way. I had to understand that God was building character. We never know what people have endured until they open their mouth to speak. Neither do we know why God chooses to bless the way he does. One can't lead anyone, anywhere, if they haven't gone through life's experiences. I refer to these experiences as the journey of life, and whatever situations each of us may confront help us serve and relate to others. We share one another's burdens. We cannot feel the pain of others if we have never experienced pain. But I remembered reading a bible passage (Isaiah 53:3) referring to Jesus as a man of sorrow acquainted with grief, and I remember that David encouraged himself in the Lord. The Bible became real to me as I had to live it by knowing grief and being encouraged by the Lord! I vowed never to return home to the land of my father. I wanted nothing to do with ministry or anything else! The hidden secrets of my dad's estate almost became the death of the family... To those **who have ever felt angry with God or betrayed, clueless, and broken-hearted** this is for you... Keep trusting. Nothing is for naught. Your labor is not in vain!

WHEN WILL IT END: Deaths of Loved Ones

Through ages 28 to 30, the winds of change began to blow. I had come into my own. I had worked doing real estate, tailoring, touring as a singer, and I definitely had no need for returning home. I received a call in January of 2000 saying my god-daughter (who was 8 years old) had passed away of heart failure. Not too long after, January 26, 2000, I received a call from my sister saying my brother was hospitalized and had died of a massive heart attack at age 45.

On March 1st, 2001, I arrived home from work (which is now my deceased brother's birthday, oddly enough), to find my sister hemorrhaging on the bathroom

Chapter 7 – Strategic Storm

floor. She had been recently diagnosed with Cystic Fibromyalgia, and something had just gone terribly wrong in her body. By the time we made it to the hospital, they could not even draw out a tube of blood to analyze. She had bled out and was flatlining on the monitor. I think I must have prayed myself nearly to death, BUT I KNEW THE GOD OF ISRAEL from childhood; for He had worked a miracle within me! So, I prayed intensely like never before in my life. My sister would go in and out of consciousness although flatlining on the monitor. The room felt unnaturally cold and shadowed with darkness. Three hours she would ride death's coattail, until an unknown doctor walked into the room. He appeared to be from an Eastern culture, maybe India. I was praying with my head in my hands. He put his hand on my shoulder before leaving the hospital room and said, "Son, whatever you are doing… keep doing it!" He left the room and all of a sudden, I see doctors and nurses flooding in to give her bloodwork and meds. (Now, beforehand they had not because why would you give a dead woman blood and meds? Who could blame them?) Even in all of the commotion, I never let my sister look back toward the monitor for fear that she would know that she was reading flatlined and lose heart in her fight to live. It is a miraculous story, one she tells in her memoir (Yes, she wrote a book about it!). God revived her from death and she is alive today to tell the story of her account. This was my experience in watching God do something so supernatural. Call it what you will, but I was there.

I never saw that doctor again. I even asked the hospital staff about him, but no one knew of any such doctor. Real doctor or not, this was my encounter with the

Chapter 7 – Strategic Storm

God of Healing and NOW He has gotten my attention! I don't think I really knew God, truly, until that moment in time and age. It was then I truly began to walk with Him.

What did God do, or allow, to drive you back to Himself? Or how did He get your attention in His relentless pursuit over you?

2002 was the year my sister-in-law passed away from congestive heart failure, or for better words, a broken heart. Her life partner and husband (my brother) had passed two years prior. My world felt like it was crashing around me! She had been a rock for many in ministry, family and life; she was a mother, sister, mentor, prophet, evangelist, teacher, pastor, and foremost, a friend of God. She was my mentor and I had learned to pray and believe by that very torch of faith and passion she carried to light the pathway for Christ. I am who I am because of her belief and trust. I know heaven received her as she passed the mantle. "All eyes on you," she said.

So, let this be written of her, my sweet sister. Thank you for the prayers and labor of love. She had been a spiritual voice and mother in ministry and she used her gift of sight to steer me as I grew up through the thorns and brambles of life. One book could not contain it all. She was one of the church mothers that prayed for me after I ingested lye. Never would I have known that she would become my sister-in-law and her missionary work would later be recommended for a Nobel Peace Prize by the President of the US).

During this time, I went through a heavy depression. I didn't know that Christians could even go through depression. I learned never to judge people because you never know the costs, sacrifices, or issues surrounding their circumstances that made them to be who they are. My

Chapter 7 – Strategic Storm

brother and his wife pastored together and now the one thing that I had told God that I wouldn't do, I now had to do because He willed it to be so! I became the interim pastor. Over the years, I had been an associate minister of their church on Saturdays. It was at their church that I preached my first initial sermon. I told you that I was called into the ministry at seventeen, but what I failed to mention is that I was not going to tell the church until much later. However, I was alone the day it was revealed to me on a Saturday morning, but God also revealed it to my sister-in-law, and she announced it from the pulpit later that same day. She stated, calling me by my middle name, (the same name God used that morning when I heard Him audibly) "God said, that He told you to preach." The church rejoiced, but I had no idea that God had told her until the moment right before she stood to minister. God used her to confirm the ministry and His voice before the congregation. However, years later, God used that moment for me to be received by the members of the church and board during my time as interim pastor. God had prepared that moment in time to carry the ministry until my next assignment. This was definitely no coincidence!

In June 2002, my dad suffered a stroke and was placed in a nursing home. During my 10 years away, God had been dealing with him and me. During the last year of his life, he called me into his room. He asked me to see about his affairs (of which I knew very little). "Most of all," he says, "take care of my girls," which meant my sister and mother. This was the first time that my dad and I ever spoke with each other and *to* each other in an actual, audible, pleasant conversation. He said, "You look like me." Over time, I had

Chapter 7 – Strategic Storm

grown facial hair and my skin had darkened, and for the first time, HE RECOGNIZED ME AS HIS SON! We sat in the nursing home and talked for a while and then he said the three magic words every child needs to hear from their father. Before leaving the nursing home, he said, "I love you."

Even now, I begin to weep (excuse the wet page) when I reflect on it. God cared that much to make sure we were reconciled. LOOK AT GOD…WOW!

My body went numb. I didn't even know how to receive this. I didn't expect it! But it was his only way to offer what he had left. While in the nursing home within that year, dad said that Jesus had visited him in a dream. He saw escalators going up and down, but he said Jesus refused to take him at that time. I understood why; because there was yet a little unfinished business between the family! Although my dad was saved, He was delivered (and so was I) when we forgave one another. I got to spend a few more moments with the man I NOW knew as my dad. In 2003, my dad passed away from congestive heart failure, but not before telling me something I needed to hear: he loved me. I didn't know I needed the healing. I did his eulogy and I told this story which God used to show HIS love. Thanks Dad!

This is to **those who have ever suffered loss** (children, parent, other family or otherwise) to **those who feel exhausted, depressed, and on auto-pilot, to the bereaved and grief-stricken, heavy-hearted with despair, and the broken relationships that seem irreparable…**

Weeping is only for a while (night) and joy does come in due season. (Psalm 30:5) Just be strong and keep

Chapter 7 – Strategic Storm

your head up. God will redeem the time! Be encouraged, you can make it through your night or storm!

Healing in the Midst of Sadness

By then, depression had really set in, but God encouraged me to write, sing, and minister. It was as if He was saying," Sing your way through." I recorded my first album. I experienced vocal nodules and I had reflux so bad that by my debut album, I was a singer that had no voice to sing. But on October 16th, 2003, the day of the debut concert, we assembled for prayer. That night a voice came out of me that I know wasn't mine. I song for two hours straight. God still showed his healing hand to make light of the enemy. I learned that it was never of my power and will, but only by His Word that we were sent to GO and do His work!

Now I was still pastoring in the interim with two churches. I had sworn to myself that I would not pastor or preach, but God willed otherwise. Oh, the humor of God! Never tell Him what you are not going to do, you may be surprised!

In the midst of grieving, I told God that I had lost my brother and my dad. One day while in devotion and meditation, I heard God prompt me, saying, "I will restore what the cankerworm has eaten or destroyed." (Joel 2:25) I asked within myself, "How on earth can you restore a dead brother and father?" Well, not three months after my dad's funeral, I received a call from a total stranger. He said, "Is this Minister Baker? I think I'm your brother." It was my half-brother from dad's "other side of the family." We made arrangements to meet. All of these years, we had never

Chapter 7 – Strategic Storm

known one another or crossed paths. But on Dec 29th, 2003, here walked a man on my porch looking like my dad and was my half-brother, a doctor from California. Wow! (I had heard of him when I was a kid through smaller conversations while eavesdropping on the adults). We looked at each other, and all we could do was just embrace one another. (If you're reading this brother, Dad was proud of you!)

This is **to those awaiting the promise of God and standing in faith with the courage to believe...** God is faithful and he has promised that he can do above what we could ever ask or think. (Ephesians 3:20)

NOW, I FELT A PROMPT FROM GOD TO GO, leave kindred and foe, and move to Georgia. By this point, I had lost five immediate family members and was moving to Georgia with my mom who has just been diagnosed with Alzheimer's Dementia Disease. I was at breakdown stage. I had to minimize my life. I didn't really need anything of my dad's, so I had already signed over everything while he was living to sustain him. I just had to finish up the remaining pieces. I sold my homes, cars, and even gave away a few. What I needed could not be purchased or sold. I needed and wanted peace! I had spent time acquiring "wealth" only to find that these "things" didn't bring the fulfillment of God's joy and peace (Ecclesiastes 5:10; Philippians 4:19). My focus changed to feel more of a burden for community, the broken and the lost (Psalm 37:4). God was maturing me to truly feel His heart.

Many are the afflictions of the righteous, BUT GOD will deliver them out of them ALL (Psalm 34:19). We search a lifetime to find OUR purpose, but we fail to find it because the purpose is HIS. It is only when we lose our life or agenda

Chapter 7 – Strategic Storm

that we can find HIS purpose and plan for our life. Only then can we cease just existing and find the true meaning in living!

Before leaving, I had the unique opportunity to minister at a prison. God had given a passage of scripture (Acts chapter 8) concerning Phillip and the eunuch who desired to be baptized. God had been prompting me to tell my story. By the time the ministry date arrived, I had determined to leave. Ashamed and yet transparent, I began preaching with my eyes closed in order not to engage anyone with eye contact for fear of judgment. What God did that night not only delivered the prisoners, but it delivered me! God proved Himself yet once again. Before opening service, I had asked the warden about what hindered the prisoners from being baptized as in the Bible story. The warden replied, "The baptismal is broken. It needs repair." Well, what do you know. It was then that I knew why God had given that scripture to me when I arrived. Before closing the message that night, I offered prayer and the invitation for salvation. I called for some water to be used to sprinkle although, I am a believer in immersion, but since the baptismal was broken, we were not hindered. I closed my eyes to pray and opened them. A line began to form as I prayed over each one individually. I closed my eyes and opened them again. Each time the line would be longer. My testimony and shame became God's glory. God used my pain for their salvation. Forty-two were added to the church that day! I had feared about what others would think when I talked about the real issues of my life as a "PK" kid. However, this was the thing that God desired to use!

Now I speak **to the healed, hopeful, the leader, and the obedient, bound by the nails in Christ's hands**

Chapter 7 – Strategic Storm

and feet (the work of the cross) but freed by the power of His resurrection.

So, I gave up what I thought I had gained.

<u>IT JUST SO HAPPENED: No Coincidence</u>

I knew how blessed I could be when surrendering to God. I cried out in a hotel room alone while on tour at a gospel conference, "God I'm tired and I can't do this anymore!" That is when God said, "Let me do it!" I was prompted to go down a street called Hurricane Shoals to find a townhouse, which just so happened was about to be vacant on March 6th, 2004. I told God, "If you want me to move or go, You have to sell my home and handle the estate." My home sold by cash in three days on February 28th, 2004. We were moved to Georgia by March 6th.

Now here is the other part of the story. I had been applying to various jobs in Georgia and landed a great one working for M' Warehouse. However, when I arrived, they said they had no recollection of me or any paperwork ever filled out for their application process. How weird was that? They promised me a tailoring position that no longer existed when I arrived. I began looking for other positions. But every time I would apply, the company or place would go on a hiring freeze. I finally tried to work for W-mart and they went on a hiring freeze the following day after applying.

In my devotion, I heard God prompting concerns about His little ones. Of course, I believed that we were about to really do something which involved an immediate job. However, He then said, "Go to school." What? When I was trying 15 years ago, we had that fiasco with my father,

Chapter 7 – Strategic Storm

and you want me to go NOW? I had tried earlier to study urban landscaping and design and now, fifteen years later, I was going to a Bible College turned University for a secular degree in Global Economics and Urban Development. Nevertheless, I enjoyed the school so much that I received three degrees. I actually found out that I liked pastoring too, but in a different way, not behind a pulpit, but by walking with real, raw people. I worked with non-profits that supported transitional homes for prisoners, homeless, and orphans. God helped me to find my passion. Over time, I began to write within these years of schooling and no work. I never knew that I could write until he sat me down from working. Out of that desert experience flowed a children's storybook and the life of my testimonies of which I share some of in this book.

During my first two years of my Associates Degree, I received enough college credits to get a job working with the county school system substitute teaching. I couldn't find a job because I had not been fully qualified to receive the one God desired to give me! Oh, the timing of God!

God wants to bless us more than we want to be blessed. He wants to bless you, but in His season and timing; wait on Him!

He sent me to work with children with behaviors. "Oh NO, not me. These are undesirables," I said. "These children hit, kick, spit, punch, curse, and everything else. God, I know this is not the job or place. There wasn't anything in the county orientation that stated this!" I walked in as a substitute teacher with the intent of quitting the next day, BUT, I HEARD GOD SAY "YOU were the undesirables I came for." He *was* concerned about His

Chapter 7 – Strategic Storm

babies. I almost missed it! So, I stayed. My pride was broken and I returned to that facility for two months before being hired on for seven more years. I actually loved working there!

During the move, I met family members in Georgia. Remember the brother who was killed before his wedding? After being invited to play pool at a friend's house, we started talking about a town called Prattsville. If you blink your eyes, you are through it, so anyone there pretty much knows you or is kindred. Come to find out, this friend was my cousin. During the time I had been traveling doing music, I was visiting the place where I would move: Atlanta, GA. I knew no one, but all of a sudden, I had found family. Then my newfound cousin called her dad and he said, "Does he know that he is in the room with his mother's grand-daughter and great-grandkids?" This was my eldest brother's children! I was playing pool with my older niece and seeing her children! She was home from serving in Afghanistan and had come over to visit my newfound cousin.

What if I had never started singing that album which later caused me to move to Georgia? I probably would have never met family. God answered prayers from my childhood and He never forgot them! He had to get me out of my comfort zone to bless me!

During the last year of college to receive my MBA, I received a call from a businessman wanting to buy my parent's property. He said he had been searching for me for about three years and he was about to give up the day I answered the phone. (He stated that he had found me through a music website.) He described the land, but I didn't know that it belonged to *my* parents. It was land that I always wished was ours. Come to find out, the deeds had been

Chapter 7 – Strategic Storm

switched by my uncle and father. The land that I played on as a child with the neighbor kids was actually my parent's property. The property was sold and I completed college and was able to open up a youth foundation.

And I suppose you were wondering how I met Mike Rodriguez? You know that children's storybook I was working on in the years of leaning on God when I couldn't find a job? Well, fast-forward some years and I will finish the story. While doing a worship night, I met two of the sweetest people: Kelly and Maggie Castor. We 'accidentally' started talking about the books we had written. They referred me to Mike. After speaking with Mike, he was prompted in the last part of our conversation to ask about writing my testimony in a co-authored book. I remind you that it all started with the children's storybook being published, *"The Animals Next Door."* Coincidence? Not really.

What I really want you to know is God's Word is true. He is Faithful. The Bible says, "The steps of a good man are ordered by God." (Psalms 37:23) Nothing is by coincidence! God has orchestrated the storms in your life to bring you to His expected end. Our "strategic storm" is a set-up for God's favor! So, when you face your storms in life, just know that you have been selected, chosen to be favored by God to be blessed. So, be blessed and highly favored! Your latter will be greater than your past!

About the Author – Addison Baker

Addison Baker is a graduate of Beulah Heights University with an MBA and a degree in Global Economics & Community Development. He serves in the community of 12Stone Church under the dynamic leadership of Pastor Kevin Myers. In addition to being an author/illustrator, he is CEO and Executive Director of Adonaijah Youth Foundation, a motivational speaker, mentor/minister, life coach and special needs educator. Although he displays a gamete of local, national and international ministry, he is passionate about the well-being of youth and community. He is a recording artist who has won 1st place Male Vocalist/Soloist with Christian Artist Talent Search. He has authored two books (latest children's storybook release- "The Animals Next Door") and has a discography of 4 CD projects: "On 1 A-chord," "I Will Praise," "It's Coming Together," and his latest- "Simple Things in Life." He has appeared on TV and in theatrical stage performances, opened for Grammy Award winning artists such as Smokie Norful and Jim Brickman, and performed for former President Bill Clinton.

Addison Baker
P.O. Box #57
Buffalo, NY 14225
addison@addisonbaker.com
www.addisonbaker.com

Chapter 7 – Strategic Storm

Chapter 8 – Reconnecting with Your Why

Chapter 8

Reconnecting with Your Why
By Josh Mercer

My story is about how I reconnected with why I wanted to be a police officer. You will learn why I wanted to be a cop and then how I lost connection with my why and ultimately, I will share the tools I used to reconnect with my purpose. I believe that these simple tools will help you as well.

Becoming a police officer had been a dream ever since I had been a kid. I had struggled and fought through some demons to become a police officer. I thought that once I became a police officer, I would be able to help real people solve real problems because of those past demons and life experiences. I had become a police officer in the first place to help people. I was born to be the sheepdog.

My mother was always loving and supportive of anything I wanted to do. However, she did not understand, and probably still doesn't understand why I would want to put myself in harm's way to help other people the way we do. I could not explain to her the urge and curiosity that runs through my veins when there is a violent action afoot. I have always been curious about violence and what makes people tick, why they do what they do. My mother is not where my struggles came from. My mother is an awesome and amazing woman who I have learned a lot from. The demons came

Chapter 8 – Reconnecting with Your Why

from my stepfather, who my mother initially wanted to fix; she is a fixer. However, the fixer cannot fix the person needing to be fixed unless they want to change. My stepfather wanted to change for a moment, but once they were married and he got what he wanted, he started to revert back to what I can only imagine was his old ways. He was a third-time divorcee and father of several who wanted nothing to do with him. This should have been a clue, but what can I say, my mom is a fixer and needed a project. She got it.

I can still hear the echoes of my stepfather's faint southern accent as he would dispense his opinion of me in his big booming voice. I can even feel his hot breath on my ear and the feel his salt and pepper goatee scraping my neck as he whispered in my ear, "You will never be good enough, you will never amount to anything." I couldn't even master grabbing the right wrench from the toolbox as he attempted to teach me the fine art of duct taping our broken down car so that it would last another week. I remember thinking: "If you just had a job then you could buy a real car and not have to fix this rattle trap." That sentence never made it out loud or I would have been crushed like a bug. We would spend weekends fixing the car and weekdays push-starting it so my mom could work to put food on the table and he could spend his days cheating on her and drinking with the neighborhood harlot.

My stepfather was a master linguist and professional cusser. He could work magic with the spoken threat and he could back it up with his 250-pound, six-foot-one frame and a solid right hook. He seemed to get more practiced as he aged and got better and more creative as time passed over

Chapter 8 – Reconnecting with Your Why

my relatively short time knowing him. My saving grace was that he did not have kneecaps and could not run. I developed a sixth sense when things started to get heated and I would edge for the door, then the driveway, and finally the woods where I would wait out his legendary Irish temper. I usually used this time in quiet contemplation about what had happened and what triggers were pushed in order to avoid any further punishment. The triggers seemed to be a moving target, so I was always searching for the trigger. I found a lot of them. I found what sparked them and what could be used to avoid them. I became a master at prevention, but even a master must practice. I practiced a lot. I learned early on to use nonverbal cues and humor to negate a beating. I started to pride myself on only getting a tongue lashing over getting the fists of furry.

The decision to become a police officer came in the form of a hammer that had missed my head by about two inches one day. My stepfather had asked that I go find it. I couldn't, he was sitting on it. He was actually sitting on a cushion with the hammer underneath it when he asked me to find the hammer. How could I be such an idiot and not know where it was? When I returned without the hammer, I advised him that it was not in the required spot. I was greeted with a snarl and flourish of polished profanity, and then the hammer met the barn door to the right of my head. I measured later; it was about two inches. The hammer didn't connect with my head, but it did leave a mental dent.

In the future, every time I messed something up, I would think of the powerful words this man hammered into my brain at ten or eleven years old, driving the mental dent into my head further and further. "You will never amount

Chapter 8 – Reconnecting with Your Why

to anything. You are not good enough. You are a loser!" I left that day and went to sit in the privacy of the woods as far from the potential beating as I could get. It was there that I made three decisions.

The first decision I made was that I was going to be something despite what he thought. I would amount to something. I was going to prove this monster wrong. Over time, this gave me focus and power, just to prove him wrong. The second decision I made was that I was not going to model myself as a father figure after this man and would have to find another way.

I found a mentor that I used as a father figure and watched as he handled difficult situations with a calm manner. He didn't know I was watching, but I was watching intently. In fact, I remember loading wood in the back of my mentor's pick-up truck one day. I valiantly tossed a round of firewood into the back of the pickup and watched in slow motion as it went through the back window. I braced for impact from my new father figure; I prepared for at least a verbal lashing. What I got was, "Oops! Are you OK?" Really? No put down, no beating? Am I OK? What manner of control and sorcery did this man have? I modeled my fatherhood after his actions instead of the learned behavior I was taught before my decision.

The final decision was that I was going to be a police officer. I had seen a demonstration at school and was in awe about what police officers did, how they did it, and why they did what they did. I also thought that it seemed like police officers liked to helped people in my kind of situation. My goal was set and my target was clear. I had no clue how to get there, but I knew what I wanted.

Chapter 8 – Reconnecting with Your Why

I realized later in life that I had not met my goal of becoming a police officer. I was disappointed in myself and old demons crept in. Questions about my manhood, achieving goals, and being good enough crept in until I replayed the mental videotape again of the hammer. I got angry, shoved them aside, plowed forward, and achieved my goal; I became a police officer.

Because of my past life experiences, I felt as though I could talk to just about anyone about anything. I could identify with everyone in almost any situation, from the homeless veteran to the child who had abusive parents to the businessman who had just lost it all or the person who wanted to end it all. I had lived it and worked through it. I was actually having a great time dealing with people and solving problems. Nothing seemed to phase me because nothing people said or did could be any worse than that of my stepfather. People couldn't touch his creative put-downs and Irish temper. On one trip to the hospital and jail one night, I actually laughed at an arrestee who was trying to cuss me out and hurt my feelings or get under my skin. I advised him that he was going to have to work harder at hurting my feelings… I had already started to build a wall. At one point, I almost felt grateful that I had gone through what I had gone through so that this part of life was easy. Almost.

What I didn't realize was that things were building up and they started from the first day on the job. People love cops when they are not getting arrested, are not in trouble, or when they need help. However, when people are being told what to do or getting arrested, the stepfather emerges in each one of them and things start stacking up in my head like

Chapter 8 – Reconnecting with Your Why

a sandwich piled too high without the supporting toothpicks. Things were soon going to topple.

The following was the moment when I lost it.

I was finishing a theft report about a block from the call that would change my view on humanity. Dispatch squawked loudly over the radio: "Information only... Fire in route... unconscious 8-year-old male ... not breathing... 315 Hawkins... information only... 1858."

I had time to flip on my lights and siren to clear one car out of the way, but I believe I made it to the front door by the time the dispatcher timed the call out at 1858 hours.

"3 Paul 78 - dispatch, arriving Hawkins... confirming 315?"

My heart stopped. There are no numbers on this house! The house to the right is 317. The house to the left is blocked, I can't see past the unruly hedges surrounding the front porch. I have been to this area before but did not memorize the house numbers. My brain was running rampant knowing that the unconscious and non-breathing child inside one of these houses may only have moments of life left in him. Dispatch had not been able to update with any information other than the house number. I made a decision and proceeded toward the house in front of me knowing that it may be the wrong one, but with the information given, this was my best chance and time was of the essence. I left my lights on to be a beacon to the fire department and other units that may be coming into the area.

Chapter 8 – Reconnecting with Your Why

I knocked loudly at the front door of a run-down, blue and white two story house with the front porch partially falling in. By the sound of it, I had the right place. There was a screaming female inside, this must be it!? I had been to the house before and knew there were several young children that lived there and a volatile, meth-infused relationship between the parents also resided inside.

"This is a possibility," I thought to myself and helped myself to the front door. Liabilities immediately ran through my mind as I announced my presence and crossed the threshold. I want to go home safe at the end of the night. I don't want to be stupid about this. Is this a trap?

"Police Department!" I yelled as I tried the door, liabilities still spidering through my brain. I knew I was doing the right thing, but I had run into accidental miscalls before and my goal is to go home at the end of the night. I could hear screaming but no answer. It sounded like a domestic violence call, but I could not understand what was being said! I was on high alert for an ambush, a male with a knife, a female with a baseball bat, a meth zombie, or anything that could be behind this door.

"3 Paul 78 - dispatch, confirming; 315 Hawkins? Are you still on the phone with them? … I'm in the house and need them to…. Found'em! Have fire and other units step it up!"

The scene was dirty. The overwhelming smell of a combination of cat urine, dog feces, and garbage punched me in the nose, almost taking my breath away. There were white styrofoam containers littering the floor and little dogs licking away at the leftovers. The shag carpet floor was blue

Chapter 8 – Reconnecting with Your Why

with a thick layer of who-knows-what brown covering it. *"How do people live like this?"* I thought to myself.

I bounded over a pile of last week's styrofoam dinner containers like a hurdler into the scene that I was just barely able to comprehend. I could see a grayish purple young man on the couch slouched over. We were in trouble.

I remember thinking, "Thank the Lord there was a seasoned dispatcher on duty that day who could multitask." This was going to go downhill fast. I know they were trying to explain CPR to the hysterical mother on the phone and listen to my barking orders plus relay to fire that I needed them there NOW!

Sitting on the couch, used as a makeshift bed, was a young man about the size of a 20 year old, extremely obese. He was surrounded by dirty laundry... or was it clean... I couldn't tell. His mother was screaming at the dispatcher, "Do something, do something, send someone, help me!" She was backed up as far as she could in the small room, huddled in the corner, petrified, frozen except for her mouth that would not stop moving. She spewed profanity like a drunken sailor who had just stubbed his toe. She was not listening to the dispatcher; she was doing all the talking, screaming emphatically for SOMEONE to do something, yet, she just stood there. We were in the dining room that had been made into a makeshift bedroom, only with oversized couches, blankets, laundry, and take-out containers covering every inch of the floor.

I held my breath and cleared the way to my target, kicking loose items and small animals out of the way to get to him. The young man was slouching on the overstuffed couch, slumped over at the neck, blubber from his neck was

Chapter 8 – Reconnecting with Your Why

protruding from his Cheeto-stained white T-shirt, rolling over his collar like a wave. His skin color was grayish blueish purplish. He wasn't breathing, and he hadn't been for a while. It didn't look good!

"Hang up!" I yelled to her. She clutched the phone tighter and clung to the furnace in the corner of the room. "HANG UP! I need your help to move him!" She was still frozen. "Fine! I'll do it myself…" I didn't know if I could move this beast, but I would find a way. I would make a way.

There was something stuck in the kid's mouth. I scraped the goo from his mouth. There was a long string of black phlegm that came out of his throat. I flung it from my fingers; it splattered on the brown velour cushion like the last glob of paint to come out of a spray paint can. Gross! I needed to get him off of the couch so I could work on the situation. Mom was still frozen and screaming for the dispatcher to do something. Her eyes were glazed over; she didn't even know I existed. I felt for her, but I needed her help to give this kid a chance.

"YOU are definitely breathing!" I thought. *"Now help me!"* …Nothing. She only clutched her phone and screamed at the dispatcher to do something. The dispatcher couldn't, she was twenty miles away. "LADY! I am right here, help me help you." Nothing!?

I grabbed his legs at the ankles and yanked to get him straightened out. Wow! This kid was heavy! I probably pulled my back out again, there goes my weekends, now I'd be going to the chiropractor and missing golf! I knew that was a selfish thought but acknowledged it as such and determined to keep going. I gave him another yank. It was like he was velcroed into the couch! I finally got his body,

Chapter 8 – Reconnecting with Your Why

and more importantly, his neck straightened. I cleared his mouth again and got the same result. I hit him on the back which cleared a large puddle of black mucus. I waited for a split second. No pulse! No breathing. I was kneeling in the mucus now while attending this kid. He needed chest compressions.

I didn't have room on the couch and it was too soft to do compressions. I needed floor space and help getting him from the couch to the living room so that when medics got there they would have a place to work. I pleaded with the mother to help me lug her son off of the couch. Nothing! Just more screaming for dispatch to do something. I am not sure if she even knew I was there.

Fine, I'll find a way! "3 Paul 78 - dispatch ... have fire step it up!" I barked orders. "The house is directly across from my car!" Was fire lost? They are taking forever! My overheads were on, you could see those things from space. Fire was less than five miles away. This was their turf. Why were they not here?

I pulled the young man off the couch feet first. His body slumped off and his head whipped in slow motion, striking the clothing that lay on the ground around the couch. I kicked the clothing from under his back to give me a flat spot to work. Again, with the black mucus! I scraped, flung, and turned him again to clear his throat. I had about an inch of clear space on either side of him. As I straddled him, I realized I would not fit over this eight-year-old. I needed room to the side. Fire should be here! They can help. Where are they!?

It was August, hot! I was carrying 50lbs of extra bulk with my outer vest carrier, gun, radio, bulletproof vest,

Chapter 8 – Reconnecting with Your Why

ammo, extra everything … but nothing that would help in this situation, just bulk. I was sweating profusely.

I got in position for chest compressions the best I could. It was not the best stance, and I teetered on his belly as I gave the first thrust. As I gave the compression a large slug of sputum erupted from his throat, hitting me in the face. Note to self: Keep your mouth shut! A drop of sweat ran down my nose and hit him in the face. Not an equal trade, but I'll take it. It's the little things!

Second compression: I thrust down with both hands, hard enough to massage his heart into submission, but I got nothing. I kept going. They say if you do it right you may crack the sternum or the ribs, but you are able to massage the heart and keep the blood flowing. That was what I was attempting to do, give him every chance to survive. Every chest compression is one closer to him making it.

That is when the moment came, in the middle of the third chest compression, about half way down. The moment is locked in my skull, frozen as a split second in time, hyper-speed and space-locked it in as the camera angle in my head circled around from every angle in that microsecond; his mother screamed, "If you hurt him, I'll sue you!"

At the time it didn't faze me. As a cop, I had heard the phrase, "I'll sue you" hundreds to thousands of times before. I just kept going with chest compressions to the beat of The Bee Gees, 'Stayin Alive,' just as I had been trained.

Fire got there. Thank God! I checked the timing afterword from my computer because it seemed like hours and I was mad. One minute, seventeen seconds after I had arrived, fire arrived on scene. It seemed like hours! Fourteen seconds later, my entire squad arrived as well. We moved him

Chapter 8 – Reconnecting with Your Why

to the living room to work on him. Myself, my partner, and Medics worked on him for forty-five minutes.

He didn't make it.

I continued my day like most other days of reports and mundane calls. It wasn't until I called my wife about 12 hours later to tell her that I wasn't going to be home on time because of some leftover paperwork. She asked the usual question, "How was your day?" All I could get out was, "I couldn't save him!" My wife is an amazing woman and she just listened. She listened to nothing as we sat in awkward silence for a while. We had not experienced this before. Usually, I would regale her with stories of laughter and fun chasing bad guys; epic battles of good triumphing over evil. However, in this moment there was no funny, no battle, no good. Just pain with no good answers.

I was scared. Affected. Traumatized. Why? What about this event got to me? This wasn't my child; it wasn't my fault. I was confused. I had seen death, dismemberment, officer-involved shootings where the officer didn't make it, train vs. human, splatter and mush, rollover accidents, gunshot wounds, knife wounds, and too many suicides to count. What about this one got to me? I tried to shake it off and bury it.

Later, this scene kept playing over and over in my head. My sleep, my being was affected. I was grumpy, sarcastic, overly sensitive, and brutally abrupt to the people I served. On the job I had turned into the stepfather I hated. I hated myself because of it, but could not shake it. I was prone to self-induced stupidity by drinking and eating too

Chapter 8 – Reconnecting with Your Why

much, doing anything to numb the mind and chase the demons away for a moment. Did this event give me some sort of Post-Traumatic Stress Disorder (PTSD)? The thought pissed me off and I would go through a cycle of grumpiness again. I began to push the event so far down in my memory that I could not remember why I was grumpy, sad, sarcastic, and unhappy. It was just a habit now. I knew that this was not the natural me, but I could not figure out why. Why was I so done? This was not me.

I didn't care anymore. I could care less about people and their stupid problems and they could tell. I actually began to hate people. I was physically sick before going to work. Arguments erupted, and fights were caused by my poor attitude. My coworkers could tell something was off. My family could tell something was way out of whack. Over the course of about six months I self-medicated with food, alcohol, and golf to the point my family didn't recognize me and I physically could not fit into my work jumpsuit any longer. In fact, I couldn't recognize me when I looked in the mirror. I was embarrassed. The Velcro on my vest carrier was stretched to the limit and if I wanted to draw my gun, I would have to work around my belly roll to do it. This was not safe! This was not me. What happened to me? I was usually a jokey smurf at work and with people on the street. Now I hated them with a passion. I didn't even like myself.

I had lost *why* I became a police officer in the first place.

I found the answer in prayer and meditation one day. Someone mentioned that meditation had helped in awakening the mind to new business solutions and I tried it.

Chapter 8 – Reconnecting with Your Why

I was attempting to find solutions to problems I couldn't comprehend.

I recognized that I had gained weight and wanted to lose it. I started working out. If you could picture a cross between a spaz and an epileptic, that was me attempting to force doughnuts, beer, and poor choices out of my pores. My meditation time was in the sauna where I would sit in silence for about twenty minutes. I tried to concentrate on breathing as I had read about, but my mind would find squirrels and I would end up mentally chasing them and not thinking about what I had planned on.

Until one day, I asked the question out loud, sitting in the privacy of my car, "God, I want to fix this. I don't want this any longer! What started this? Why do I not care anymore?" Simple, short, to the point, and real. In fact, I had yelled it! I may have cussed, but I was as real and raw as I could get. God was not paying any attention to my mumbling under my breath, so I made sure he heard and paid attention. I was mad. Not mad at God, although the thought crossed my mind. I was mad at myself for not being able to figure this thing out by myself and on my own terms, just like I had figured out so many other things in life. I believed I could only trust myself because I was the only person (other than my wife) who had not failed me.

I then proceeded to work my muscles to the point of extreme exhaustion. I was so tired that I just sat down in a puddle of sweat just before dry heaving over a nearby garbage can. I brushed off the stares and laughter in the gym, I didn't care. I had nothing left. I was done. I limped to the dressing room and sat in the sauna, nursing my self-inflicted

Chapter 8 – Reconnecting with Your Why

wounds when the answer came. It jolted me, worse than fifty thousand volts from a taser.

Bam! There it was! My answer: one sentence from a scared, frantic, helpless mother who didn't have the training or experience to help her helpless son. One sentence from a mother who meant me no harm. I was not arresting her or challenging her, I was trying with all my might to help her. "If you hurt him, I will sue you!" I immediately forgave her for her sentence, and I broke. At that moment, I was sitting in a public men's sauna at my gym, naked, crying, and crossing my fingers that someone would not enter and see the tough guy leaking from his eyes. I remember thinking that I wished I had asked the question when I was home and in a private place, so be careful what you ask for and when, because ultimately the answers do not arrive on your timeline.

I work as a police officer, but for several years I have been a paid speaker. I give classes on self-defense, workshops, seminars, and even keynotes on violence and how to avoid violence using some of the tools police officers use. I teach classes on how to think like a police officer so that you can go home safe each night to your family. I teach using my own life experiences and stories, even parts with my stepfather, including a funny interpretation of how he would try to run after me without kneecaps. No problem. However, I could not talk out loud about this experience without losing it, blubbering like a little baby.

I found a mentor and expert who advised me that quite often, PTSD comes from not being able to solve a problem. You relive the issue over and over because your brain needs to solve the problem to move on. He stated why

Chapter 8 – Reconnecting with Your Why

I was reliving the moment and I could see outside my body in a 360 camera view. I was searching for the answer to save the child. He told me that I would probably never find the answer, but recommended that I start helping myself by working through the following strategies and stop beating myself up.

I learned to stop reflecting on the past and start looking to the future, planning for the future, and moving forward. The future has promise, the past has pain.

The following are some simple nuggets that have helped me to heal and reconnect with my 'why'. I started with a pen and paper for some of them and have slowly graduated them into just the way I live. I use all of them but pick the ones that work for you to get you to where you want to go.

1. Get Grateful: Have an attitude of gratitude. Get up in the morning and be grateful for something! You are alive. You're breathing. You're healthy. Pick something other than your nose, and be grateful for it. It will change everything.

I got up in the morning and would force myself to write down simple things that made me smile. These were the first items on my list when I started: I am grateful for my wife, I am grateful for healthy kids, I am grateful to have legs that work, I am grateful to have a good sense of humor… now be funny!

I am now grateful that I made the grateful list. I am even grateful that I am snarky and have a self-deprecating sense of humor. When I get down on myself, I will still take a moment and write a list to force myself to be grateful. I am so grateful for that stupid list!

Chapter 8 – Reconnecting with Your Why

2. Have A Target to Improve: Choose to improve something in your life and work on it with curiosity and passion. Whether it's weight loss, public speaking, relationships, or focused attention on one area of life, develop a target and a plan to achieve your goal by a specific date.

I used simple and achievable targets at first. I chose to lose sixty pounds in five-pound achievable targets and gave them all a date. I chose to go to Mexico with my wife without the kids. I chose to put together a woman's self-defense class to help women fight back. I donate this class to churches and organizations who hire me to help them put together Active Shooter plans of action and safety teams. This is a way for me to give back and a way for churches to reach out to their communities.

3. Have Fun: Have fun with life. We are far too serious about our goals and ambitions sometimes. Keep it simple, have fun, smile, and laugh. You deserve to take a break from the drama of "self-improvement" and have fun.

I love to laugh. I love life and I love golf, most of the time I am laughing at my golf game, so it is a good combination. They say that laughter is the best medicine, so laugh often and laugh hard, even about the hard things in life. Laughter will correct your course and right your ship.

4. Give Yourself Permission: My mentor demanded that I give myself permission to be powerful, achieve more, do more, live more, have more fun, and stop the self-doubt.

We are told so many times that we need to have permission to do things, but we are unsure of who to ask for it. Ask yourself, but if you need to ask someone else, then

Chapter 8 – Reconnecting with Your Why

ask me. I will tell you that; I am giving you permission to be what you want to be. Be powerful. Feel free to achieve what you have set out to do. Do more with your life. Achieve the success that you have dreamt of. I give you permission to love your spouse with passion. Live your life with passion. Work toward your dreams and have more fun.

5. Make Mistakes: Give yourself permission to make mistakes. Learn and improve from your mistakes. Learn from your failures, laugh about them, and move on.

The first time I spoke in front of a group of people I lost my notes, lost the sale, and lost the respect of the church I was talking to. But I walked next door and nailed the presentation, made the sale, and gained their respect.

The first time I grappled with someone in the Jiu Jitsu Gym I attended, I was twisted in a pretzel by a girl half my age and a quarter my size. I was embarrassed but learned and improved. I could have quit, but I got curious and passionate about learning. I learned from my mistakes and now I don't let little girls beat me up anymore.

6. Share: Share what you are doing with others. You never know when your success or failures may affect the people around you. Others will use your story to either avoid making your mistakes or learn from your success. Regardless, the act of teaching and sharing will increase your ability to help others. Either way, you are helping. So feel good about yourself, keep going, keep learning, and keep sharing.

7. Exercise:

If you look up on YouTube how to exercise you will spend the next few months being confused. You will not accomplish anything, and you will be discouraged. Instead, this is my recommendation: 1. Join a gym. 2. Work up a sweat

Chapter 8 – Reconnecting with Your Why

by walking, running, biking, or something aerobic, but sweat a little. 3. Lift some light things a bunch of times and then lift some heavy things a few times. When you feel your muscles starting to burn, stop. Go take a shower and call it a day. Do it again tomorrow and for the next 21 days. I know you will skip some. Forgive yourself and keep going. I know you will pick up a doughnut or eat an extra slice of pizza. The gym is not actually for your muscles, it is for your brain. You will focus more, achieve more, and do more if you spend about twenty to thirty minutes exercising. A byproduct of working out is that you will begin to lose the muffin top and you will actually begin to look like you feel.

After you have exercised for a while with no plan and want to get complicated, feel free to hire a coach, buy a book, and watch YouTube all you want, but don't over complicate your initial action of going to the gym. If you think about it too hard you are doing something wrong. You can always over complicate things later, for now, keep it simple.

8. Pray and Meditate:

This is probably the scariest thing to give up and do, but once you do it will change your life for the positive. Praying out loud will impact your future so freakishly fast you will not be able to recognize yourself in a very short amount of time.

This is probably the most important, which is why I saved it for last. It is really simple: Ask God what you want out loud and with passion, then be prepared to receive it. The answers will come. God answers prayers, although it may not be how you want them to be answered. Relief will get to you. The time has come for you to achieve greatness. All you have to do is ask.

Chapter 8 – Reconnecting with Your Why

Using the tools above I have not only regained why I wanted to be a police officer, but I have also started to train others on how to be police officers by becoming one of our department's field training officers. I go to work every day with passion and excitement for the job. I have fun now because I reconnected with my '*why*'. My '*why*' is to help people. I am addicted to it.

Additionally, I have stepped out in faith and started speaking more frequently. I hope to be able to travel internationally to teach and train people on how to avoid violence. Using the tools I have talked about and my addiction to helping people, I have refocused my attention on helping civilian businesses share with their workers how to think like police officers, develop a 360 awareness of their surroundings, and use mental self-defense methods to go home safe to their families.

Chapter 8 – Reconnecting with Your Why

About the Author – Josh Mercer

Josh Mercer is an experienced Police Officer who delivers powerful workshops, seminars and keynotes that give you the tools you need if you are involved in an unexpected situation. Josh sees violence daily and is driven to prevent it, as opposed to reporting it. Because of his experience with law enforcement, Josh has a passion to help others. He takes pride in providing the best personalized service possible. In addition to his primary job duties, Josh has been recognized for a life-saving award and he helps train other officers in his department.

Josh has an extraordinary commitment that he calls "an addiction" to helping people. He has fostered this desire into a talent for helping people to learn how to stay safe.

Josh teaches people how to think "like police officers" in his workshops, seminars and keynotes. He teaches proven techniques to people just like you, that can be used immediately. You will go home from one of his workshops knowing that you have the upper hand in a violent situation and you will learn how you can proactively deter most situations from happening.

Josh works with public safety, civilian companies and churches taking the blindfold off violence; empowering people to be safe and live empowering lives.

Chapter 8 – Reconnecting with Your Why

You can find out more about Josh Mercer or learn how to book him for your event on his website: www.thinklikeacopseminars.com. If you want to contact him for his services, you can contact his manager directly at: booking@thinklikeacopseminars.com

If you enjoyed reading this chapter, keep an eye out for Josh's full book coming out in early 2019.

A Journey to Hope – Stories That Inspire

A Journey to Hope – Stories That Inspire

Final Thoughts

Throughout my life, I have always felt a bigger and better plan for my life, but I have not always been in pursuit of it, mostly because I have been my biggest obstacle. I was often distracted by my current comfort zones through my current routines. They kept me from stepping into my full potential and kept me bound, as a prisoner of mediocrity. I knew that I wanted to pursue my "better plan," I just wasn't focused enough to see it or empowered enough to take action.

After years of very strong feelings that God had something more for me, I only took action to start changing my life, when I chose to have faith and act on God's plan for me. I knew this was the only way to make big changes in my life.

Through His grace, I am a new man. I understand my purpose and I am full of life. I can see Him clearly, and I am stronger than ever.

With regard to purpose, I have always felt that mine was to help others through the gift of speaking. I have always dreamed of becoming a motivational/inspirational speaker, or maybe even a preacher, but for the largest part of my life, I only considered this a dream.
Who was I to do these things?
What credentials or gifts did I have?
These were negative thoughts that I burdened myself with.

So, who am I?
I am a son of our King.

I know Him and He knows me.

Today, all because of Him, and through my obedience to decide, take action and have faith, I am continuing to live my life's dream. I am pursuing my life's goal, and most importantly, my life's purpose to help others build their lives all for the glory of God. Not only do I travel and speak full-time, but I am also pursuing my MDiv at SWBTS to preach around the world.

Believe in God and accept Him and His calling for your life. Have faith and act. You too can realize your better plan as the son or daughter of the same King!

Now Go Forth and Make YOUR Life Exceptional!

- **Mike Rodriguez**

A Journey to Hope – Stories That Inspire

A Journey to Hope – Stories That Inspire

About Mike Rodriguez

Mike Rodriguez is a professional speaker, a master trainer and a global evangelist. He is CEO of Mike Rodriguez International, LLC, a professional speaking, training and global ministry organization. Besides being a Best-Selling author, he is a highly sought-after motivator and a leadership, change, and sales expert. Mike and his wife Bonnie also own a publishing company and they still manage to spend quality time with their five daughters, all while Mike is studying for his Master's Degree (MDiv). Mike previously studied at DTS (in 2017), and at SWBTS (2018). Mike is a former showcase speaker with the original Zig Ziglar Corporation and was selected as their key speaker for the 2015 Ziglar U.S. Tour.

Mike delivers performance-based seminars and trainings and has authored several books which have been promoted by Barnes & Noble. He has been featured on CBS, U.S. News & World Report, Success Magazine, Fast Company and Business Insider. He has lectured at Baylor University, UNT, K-State Research and UGA. His clients include names like Hilton, Bank of America, McDonald's Corporation, the U.S. Army, and the Federal Government. As a people expert, Mike has trained thousands around the world.

Everyone faces challenges; Mike believes that through faith and action, you can overcome the challenges in your life to attain your goals and become who God has called you to be.

Mike has been happily married since 1991 to Bonnie, the love of his life and together they have five beautiful daughters.

A Journey to Hope – Stories That Inspire

A Journey to Hope – Stories That Inspire

As a highly sought-after speaker,
Mike has experience working with people
from all walks of life.

You can schedule Mike Rodriguez
to speak, inspire or train at your next event.
Go to:
www.MikeRodriguezInternational.com

Other products available by Mike Rodriguez:

Finding Your WHY

8 Keys to Exceptional Selling

Break Your Routines to Fix Your Life

Lion Leadership

Think BIG Motivational Quotes

Walking with Faith

A Bigger Purpose

Trusting in Him

and

The Power of Breaking Routines
(Audio Course from Nightingale Conant)

A Journey to Hope – Stories That Inspire

A Journey to Hope – Stories That Inspire

A Journey to Hope – Stories That Inspire

A Journey to Hope – Stories That Inspire

Disclaimer & Copyright Information

Some of the events, locales, and conversations have been recreated from memories. In order to maintain their anonymity, in some instances, the names of individuals and places have been changed. As such, some identifying characteristics and details may have changed.

Although the authors and publishers have made every effort to ensure that the information in this book was correct at press time, the authors and publishers do not assume and hereby disclaim any liability to any party for any loss, damage, or disruption caused by errors or omissions, whether such errors or omissions result from negligence, accident, or any other cause. Each author is responsible for the content of each story.

All quotes, unless otherwise noted,
are attributed to the respective Authors or to the Holy Bible.

Cover illustration, book design, and production
Copyright © 2018 by Tribute Publishing LLC
www.TributePublishing.com

"Go Forth and Make Your Life Exceptional" ™
is a copyrighted trademark of the Author, Mike Rodriguez.

Scripture references are copyrighted by www.BibleGateway.com
which is operated by the Zondervan Corporation, L.L.C

A Journey to Hope – Stories That Inspire

*"I can do ALL THINGS through Christ
who strengthens me."
Philippians 4:13*

NOTES

NOTES

NOTES

www.ingramcontent.com/pod-product-compliance
Lightning Source LLC
Chambersburg PA
CBHW020422010526
44118CB00010B/374